Bold Colour, Texture & Design on the Frame Loom

Contemporary Weaving

Allyson Rousseau

stashBOOKS.

an imprint of C&T Publishing

Publisher: Amy Barrett-Daffin
Creative Director: Gailen Runge
Senior Editor: Roxane Cerda
Editor: Madison Moore
Cover/Book Designer: April Mostek
Production Coordinator: Zinnia Heinzmann
Illustrator: Mary Flynn
Photography Coordinator: Lauren Herberg
Photography Assistant: Rachel Ackley
Front cover photography by Isaac Vallentin
Photography by Allyson Rousseau, unless otherwise noted

Published by Stash Books, an imprint of C&T Publishing, Inc.,
P.O. Box 1456, Lafayette, CA 94549

Library of Congress Cataloging-in-Publication Data

Names: Rousseau, Allyson, 1993- author.
Title: Contemporary weaving : bold colour, texture & design on the frame loom / Allyson Rousseau.
Description: Lafayette, CA : Stash Books, an imprint of C&T Publishing, [2023] | Summary: "Dive into eye-catching contemporary weaving, perfect for anyone that loves color, textiles, and learning something new. Both beginners and advanced weavers will learn to craft their own designs and make a variety of fine art projects, like wall hangings, pillows, and coasters, that bring home decor to the next level"-- Provided by publisher.
Identifiers: LCCN 2022036236 | ISBN 9781644033050 (trade paperback) | ISBN 9781644033067 (ebook)
Subjects: LCSH: Hand weaving. | Hand weaving--Patterns.
Classification: LCC TT848 .R656 2023 | DDC 746.1/4041--dc23/eng/20220819
LC record available at https://lccn.loc.gov/2022036236

Printed in China

10 9 8 7 6 5 4 3 2 1

DEDICATION

For all my fellow weavers and weavers-to-be.

And for Isaac, my partner in life and love, for cheering me on throughout all of my creative successes and roadblocks over the past nine years. I would not be who I am or where I am today without your support (and great ideas).

ACKNOWLEDGMENTS

I'd like to thank LDH Scissors, Balfour & Co, Gist Yarns, and Weaver House for generously supplying a selection of tools and materials to help me write this book.

Endless gratitude to Madison Moore, my editor, without whom this book would not exist.

Contents

Introduction

Photo by Isaac Vallentin

What Is a Weaving?

The most traditional definition might say that it's a piece of cloth made up of a warp and a weft.

WARP is a set of vertical strings anchored to a loom, under pressure, that maintains even tension.

WEFT is everything woven in between the warp, loosely or tightly, and is usually a type of fibre.

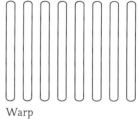

Warp

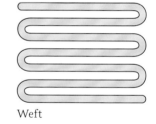

Weft

But in actuality, a weaving doesn't have to be woven with yarns or threads, and the warp doesn't have to be under pressure with the tension evenly maintained. You can weave just about anything together with some version of a warp and a weft.

You can weave with grass, clay, paper, metal—you name it. And you don't even really *need* a loom.

For me, weaving is a very good friend. Loyal, forgiving, patient, and predictable.

For some, weaving can be a kind of meditation—an activity that's practiced in solitude with great focus, that is as quiet as the sounds of their hands moving across the loom.

When I was first learning to weave, I fumbled my way through the motions, a little frustrated when one thing or another went wrong and not entirely sure why my weaving usually looked *worse* the second I started cutting it off of the loom. But weaving became easier over time, and with a few years of practice, the tension and look of my weaves really improved. The relationship I had with my loom changed too: into something of comfort. The more I wove, the more confidence I gained in my ability to produce an interesting piece of art without meeting any technical issues along the way.

Photo by Isaac Vallentin

All of the techniques, tips, and recommendations in this book are based on the past seven years of my own daily weaving art practice. I taught myself these techniques and solidified them into habits, and now they are present in every weaving I make. The tips are little nuggets of helpful information that I hope will make your journey a little smoother than my own. And everything that I recommend is an honest suggestion or shortcut that I have successfully tested many times over.

Each of the seven projects I have included has a unique technique or quality that I hope will help you apply and practice everything I share in Chapters 1 through 7. The instructions were designed in a way that enables you to re-create the project exactly as the images show while still leaving opportunities for some modifications based on your own tools, materials, and personal style.

While this book is all about weaving with yarn on a frame loom (my specialty), it's important to me to convey that weaving doesn't mean only one thing. The possibilities of what you can create are truly endless, and you don't need a lot to get started. If you take away nothing else from reading this book, I hope that my words inspire you to experiment beyond its pages and to find out what weaving means for you.

CHAPTER 1
Tools and Materials

There is an amazingly wide range of tools and materials available today that can be used for weaving, which may make you feel intimidated and confused as a beginner weaver.

For me, the beauty of frame loom weaving is that you don't need very much of anything. The information provided in this chapter will help to demystify the process and give you a guide to gather what you need for your first weaving.

The tools and materials in this book are what I use on a daily basis, and I have found them to be more than suitable for weaving on a frame loom.

Weaving Needles

Weaving or tapestry needles are characterised by long eyes (a.k.a. the hole the thread or yarn goes through) and blunt points. They range in length and thickness from size #26, the smallest, to size #13, the largest.

Some needles have bent ends. These can make it easier to ensure that you don't miss any warp threads as you're weaving, but a straight needle works just as well with a bit of patience and practice.

I have always used steel tapestry needles that are about 2¾" (7cm) long (size #13) for weaving my work. I briefly gave plastic needles a try when I first started out but realised that they were not strong or sturdy enough to withstand several hours of weaving every day.

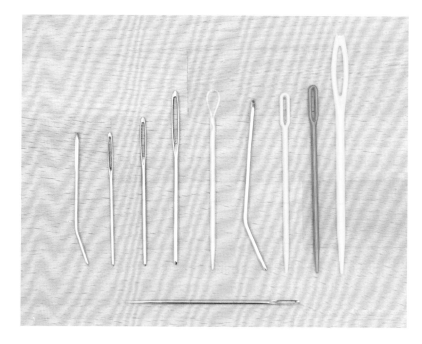

Plastic needles can work great if you're weaving a less dense weave with thicker yarns at a leisurely pace. They're good for beginner weavers who are just starting to get the feel of weaving, and they might be easier to hold than metal because plastic needles are typically a bit longer. But if you're looking for a sturdier and more versatile needle, stick with steel.

Chenille needles (pictured horizontally above) are a lot like sewing needles because they have sharp tips, but they also have long eyes like weaving needles. These are great for weaving in yarn ends on the back of your work. See Securing Yarn Ends (page 70).

You can find tapestry or weaving and chenille needles in your local craft supply stores or online.

Weaving Combs

Weaving combs help you keep your weft lines neat, evenly spaced, and pushed tightly together.

This is the tool that you will use second most often after the weaving needle.

The kind of comb you should use is dependent on the type of loom you're using, the number of warp strings per inch of weaving space, and your overall preference.

There are fancy and beautiful combs made and marketed specifically for weaving, but the funny thing is, an inexpensive hair comb will work just as well. Using whatever you already have at home is a great place to start.

The more you weave, however, the more interested you may become in finding that perfect little *weaving* comb.

I love combs made of wood. Wood is such a lovely material to touch and use because it absorbs the oils from your skin and, over time, develops a nice patina, which actually can make it stronger and better with age. I suggest that you look for one with thin teeth that aren't too far apart. The closer together your warp strings are, the closer the teeth of the comb should ideally be. This is something that will become intuitive to you the more you weave.

Combs of all kinds can be found online in a variety of sizes and materials. I recommend looking on Etsy and trying out something wooden and handmade.

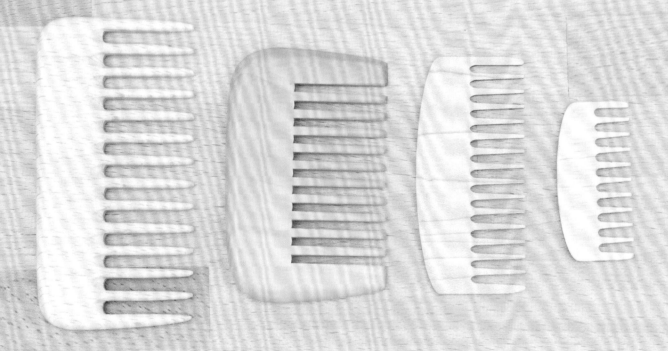

BEATERS

Weaving beaters are essentially combs with longer handles. They often are made out of wood or a combination of wood for the handle and metal for the teeth. The larger they are, the bigger the weaving, tapestry, or floor rug they're meant for.

Beaters are great for large tapestries with thin fibres and very tight weaves. Because of their larger sizes, beaters sometimes can be weighted, which allows the weaver to easily apply more pressure on the weft without having to exert more physical energy. All of these traits make the beater a beloved and necessary tool for weavers working on large floor looms that are bigger than the weavers themselves.

A comb will be better suited to make all of the projects in this book, but if you're hoping to scale up your weavings in the future, a beater might be something you'd like to add to your kit. I would recommend starting with something small and lightweight (preferably made of wood). The Woolery has a great tiny beater that is perfect for weaving on a small frame loom, but there is also a variety to be found on Etsy.

A FORK

I would be remiss not to mention this equally suitable and most accessible comb alternative: the fork. A kitchen fork is essentially a small beater and will work just like the tools mentioned above.

If you're not certain about which type of comb to buy after reading this section, I recommend starting with whatever you already own. A hair comb will give you a good idea of what it's like to use a weaving comb, and a fork will give you a good sense of what a beater feels like. You may decide that you don't need to buy anything after all!

Scissors

Having a good pair of *sharp* scissors or shears is as crucial to weaving as it is to any other fibre- or fabric-related craft. If you want to keep scissors sharp for a long period of time, it's important that you use them only on fibres. The first time you use them to cut paper, you will rapidly expedite the dulling process.

If you're like me and you use scissors all day long, I recommend having a different pair for each task...even though it may seem silly! I have a pair that I use only on paper and tape when I'm wrapping orders, another pair that I use only for cutting pieces of yarn as I'm weaving, another pair with offset handles that I sometimes use when I'm trimming raised elements in my work, and a few smaller pairs that are great for detail work. I could go even further and say that I have another pair that stays in the kitchen, another pair that stays in the workshop, and so forth, but you get the idea.

If you need just one good trusty pair that will carry you through all of your weaving projects, I recommend the 8″ (20.3cm) Midnight Edition Fabric Shears or the 6″ (15.2cm) Imperial Scissors, both by LDH Scissors.

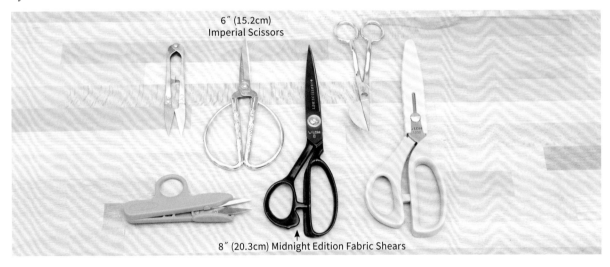

6″ (15.2cm)
Imperial Scissors

8″ (20.3cm) Midnight Edition Fabric Shears

Measuring Tools

I use a soft measuring tape that shows millimetres, centimetres, and inches. This tool is necessary for measuring nail spacing, the width of the warped space, and the length of the woven progress. A ruler will work well too.

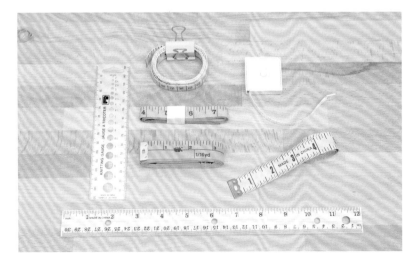

Yarn Types

DETERMINING FIBRE CONTENT

There are many types of fibres used in the textiles of today. When it comes to weaving, certain fibres are better suited to some projects than to others.

All yarns that you buy brand new will be labelled with their fibre contents. A lot of yarns are made up of fibre blends consisting of two or more types, like wool and nylon, for example. Adding nylon to wool adds strength and decreases the amount of stretch it has.

Determining the fibre content of yarns that you buy secondhand (and often without labels) can be tricky. The more you work with yarn, the better you will get at noticing details about a certain type of fibre. This accumulated knowledge will help you figure out the fibres in an unlabeled mystery yarn.

You could also do a burn test. Cut a small piece of the yarn, and burn one end. The speed at which it burns and the way it smells will give you clues. A fast-burning yarn is likely to be made of a synthetic fibre, either 100% synthetic or a blend, and a slower-burning yarn is likely to include natural fibres such as sheep's wool, for example.

Various charts can be found online that show these tests and their results in more detail if you're interested. I've included a bit of information about the notable characteristics of popular yarn fibres in this chapter to help guide you. It's not always necessary to know your yarn's exact fibre content; it's more important to understand its characteristics.

My favourite fibre types to use in weaving are cotton and wool because they are long lasting and durable!

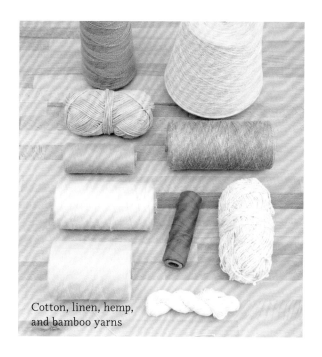

Cotton, linen, hemp, and bamboo yarns

PLANT FIBRES

COTTON: Made from cotton plant; very soft and durable fibre; excellent fibre for warping.

LINEN: Made from flax plant; very strong and absorbent; drying time is faster than cotton's, making it an excellent fibre for weaving kitchen linens; great fibre for warping.

HEMP: Made from cannabis plant; the texture is similar to linen; great fibre for warping.

BAMBOO: Made from bamboo plant; often very soft and may be blended with other types of fibres for this reason.

Alpaca, mohair, sheep's wool, and silk yarns

Thrifted mystery yarns, likely acrylic

ANIMAL FIBRES

SHEEP AND LAMB'S WOOL: The most commonly used animal fibre; warm, insulating, water resistant, and durable.

MERINO SHEEP'S WOOL: Wool from the Merino breed of sheep that produces a very fine, soft fibre; warm, insulating, water resistant, and durable.

ALPACA: Wool from the alpaca, an animal similar to and often confused with the llama; soft, warm, and durable like sheep's wool.

MOHAIR: Hair from the angora goat (not to be confused with the angora rabbit, which produces angora wool); known for its high sheen and luster; often used in fibre blends to add these qualities to the yarn.

SILK: Produced by certain insect larvae in the creation of their cocoons; very soft, shiny, and durable; one of the strongest natural fibres, though it loses a lot of strength when wet; can attract damage-causing insects.

NOIL: The short fibres left over from spinning silk or combing wool.

HUMAN-MADE FIBRES

Synthetic yarns are often available in a wider range of bright colours than are plant or animal fibres. I try my best to avoid using synthetic or "plastic" fibres in my work, but buying them secondhand is a good way to help recycle these types of fibre since you aren't directly supporting their production.

ACRYLIC: Synthetic; essentially a plastic fibre; cheaper alternative to sheep's wool; highly flammable, water resistant, and a large contributor to microplastics pollution.

POLYESTER: Synthetic; essentially a plastic fibre; highly stain and water resistant; like acrylic, highly flammable and a large contributor to microplastics pollution.

Yarn Weights

There are eight recognized yarn weights that range from Lace to Jumbo. These are most useful to know for other types of fibre arts and crafts, such as crochet and knitting, and aren't particularly crucial to weaving. I've included them nonetheless to use as a reference tool in case they come in handy for sourcing yarn.

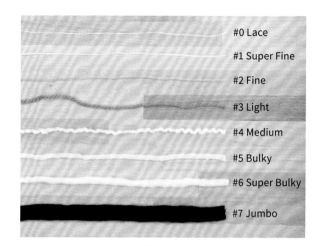

#0 Lace
#1 Super Fine
#2 Fine
#3 Light
#4 Medium
#5 Bulky
#6 Super Bulky
#7 Jumbo

Yarn for the Warp

Remember, the warp is the yarn that runs vertically between the nails of the loom. See page 48 in Chapter 4, Warping the Loom, to learn more about warping.

The number one rule in choosing warping yarn is that it cannot have any stretch. This means that when you hold a piece of yarn, one end in each hand, and pull, it doesn't stretch under the pressure. If you use a stretchy yarn for the warp, the weaving will become loose on the loom while you're working, and when it's cut off the loom, it will flop out of shape. You'll lose all your hard work (and patience).

Plant fibres (particularly cotton, hemp, and linen) are often best for the warp because of their strength and rigidity. I usually use white yarn for the warp.

My five current favourite yarns for warping are:

1. Gist Yarn 8/8 unmercerized brassard 100% cotton yarn

2. Weaver House 100% linen slub, Natural

3. Patons Hempster 55% hemp and 45% cotton blend yarn

4. Bernat Handicrafter 100% cotton yarn

5. Lily Sugar 'n Cream 100% cotton yarn

In general, look for cotton, linen, or hemp that is midweight and strong.

Yarn for the Weft

Remember that the weft is the yarn you weave horizontally through the warp. You can use any yarn type and weight for the weft on a frame loom, though some are better for certain projects than are others.

Thinner yarns are better suited to smaller weavings and can produce finer details in things like bookmarks and necklaces. Comparatively, using thicker or bulkier yarns for floor rugs will contribute to their longevity. Weaving with thin yarn will take more time and the result will appear more dense compared to thick yarn.

The spacing of the warp strings affects which yarn you can use for the weft. If the warp spacing is tight, meaning the strings are close together, you have to choose a thin weft yarn to weave with. A weft yarn that is a similar weight to or thinner than the warp yarn will be best. This warp-to-weft ratio will ensure that the warp strings are covered up.

The same rule works in reverse for heavier yarns. The wider the warp spacing (if you warp your loom around every other nail, for example), the easier it will be to weave with bulky weft yarns.

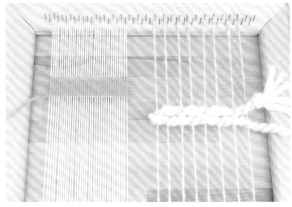

Tight warp with thin weft vs. wide warp with thick weft

Highly textured novelty weft yarns

Yarn at a thrift store

Sourcing Yarn Sustainably

My favourite way to find yarns is by thrifting them. Most of the yarns I use have been found by my own luck or thrifted for me by friends and family. There is nothing more exciting than turning the corner and spotting a brightly coloured yarn cone from across the store. What makes thrifted yarns so special to me (aside from the affordable price) is each one may be the only yarn or thread of that particular colour that I'll ever come across. I love this element of rarity in my work because it truly makes each weaving feel like one of a kind. Once I run out of a thrifted yarn, that's it; it's gone for good.

Other great places to find yarn secondhand are yard sales, church sales, and websites like Craigslist, Kijiji, eBay, and Facebook Marketplace.

When I lived in Montréal a couple of years ago, there was a church near my apartment that had a fundraising sale once a month. Every time I went to the sale, there were massive bags of yarn balls that had been hand wound by the lovely elderly lady volunteers of the church. If a sweater had been donated with a hole or a stain on it, they unraveled the sweater and wound the yarn into balls for reusing. I love this. It was such a wonderful example of how we can help to recycle and lessen our waste in the fashion and textile industries.

Another great way to find yarn without going to the store is by asking friends and family if they have any yarn in their homes that they aren't using anymore. You could even arrange for a craft night where you get together and do a yarn swap.

When Buying Yarn Secondhand...

Be sure to closely inspect the yarns and only buy ones that look clean and free from dirt and dust. Dusty or dirty yarn could leave a dark line or section in your weaving.

If you're lucky enough to find natural-fibre (plant or animal) yarn secondhand, it's a good idea to place it in a bag in your freezer for a few days to kill any possible moths (or their young) that may be hiding in the fibres.

If you can't find yarns secondhand or would rather buy them new, shopping small and supporting your local yarn shops and farms is the next best thing. Whether that means visiting the shop or farm in person or ordering online, I encourage you to support independently owned businesses and folks in your own community.

After all, half the fun of working with yarn is being creative in the ways that you collect it!

The cost of buying yarn from local shops and farms is certainly higher than the cost of thrifting it, but if you buy half of your yarn secondhand and the other half from a local shop/farmer, it will probably average out to be what you would spend if you bought all of your yarn from a big box store.

Cozy and content sheep at Lismore Sheep Farm and Wool Shop in River John, Nova Scotia

If you must buy new yarn from a big box craft or art supply store, stick to recycled and natural or organic fibres as much as you can. Better yet, see if the label says where the yarn comes from. The shorter the distance it has to travel to reach you, the smaller its carbon footprint will be, making it a more eco-friendly choice.

CHAPTER 2
The Frame Loom

Why the Frame Loom?

A frame loom is a square or rectangular frame, usually made out of canvas stretcher bars or wood, with nails, notches, or pegs on the top and bottom.

I have been using a frame loom since the day I started weaving seven years ago. I've tried a few other types of looms out of curiosity, and after each one, I found myself returning to my trusted frames with more devotion than before. There are so many benefits to weaving this way.

Photo by Isaac Vallentin

ACCESSIBILITY

The frame loom is the most all-around accessible type of loom for weaving.

A frame loom that you make yourself is possibly *the* most cost-effective loom available. If you have access to a hammer, the total cost of supplies (four canvas stretcher bars and a box of nails) will total between $10 and $15. Frame looms give you the ability to own many looms of various sizes for very little money. Locating all of the necessary loom-making materials is easy; most can be found at your local art supply, craft, and hardware stores—such as Michaels, DeSerres, and Home Depot—or online.

I make all of my looms from four canvas stretcher bars. Canvas stretcher bars are pieces of wood with slots on both ends that are made to fit into each other. This feature eliminates the need to nail or staple them together. Stretcher bars aren't always easy to find in person in the size you're looking for, but they're widely available online.

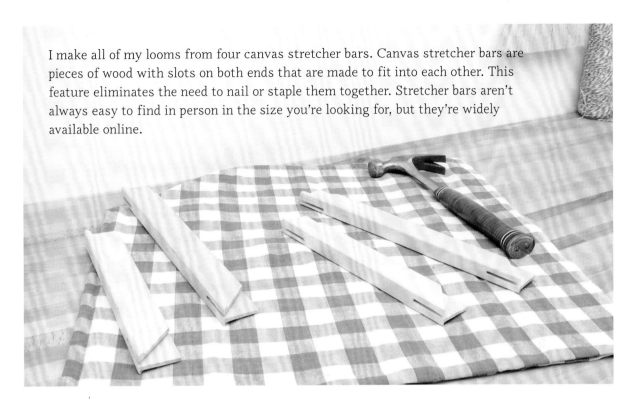

If you'd prefer to shop or source all your materials in person but can't find individual stretcher bars, there are a few alternatives that work great too. You can buy a ready-made painting canvas and pull off the gessoed canvas material that's stapled to the frame. Though more expensive, this option is great in a pinch because the frame is already assembled. Keep in mind that the thickness, type, and quality of the wood used for these frames will vary, so a loom made this way may not be as solid and long-lasting as a loom made from scratch.

If you have access to some scrap wood and a few tools, you could build a frame loom the old-fashioned way—with raw materials! These can be smooth and pretty if you'd like or rough and clunky. The way the loom looks isn't directly connected to its weaving potential. The only thing that matters is that it's sturdy and comfortable to touch.

TIP | IF YOU'VE NEVER WOVEN ANYTHING AND YOU'RE UNSURE IF IT'S SOMETHING YOU'D ENJOY, THERE ARE SOME CREATIVE ALTERNATIVES YOU CAN TRY BEFORE COMMITTING TO A LOOM. TAPING AND WRAPPING YARN AROUND A PIECE OF CARDBOARD OR A BOOK IS ONE EXAMPLE. LATER, WE'LL TRY WEAVING DIRECTLY THROUGH A PIECE OF THICK PAPER WITH A LARGE SEWING NEEDLE (SEE WEAVING WITH YARN ON PAPER, PAGE 39).

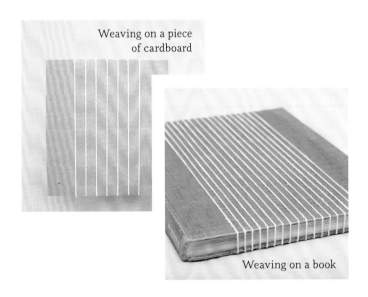

Weaving on a piece of cardboard

Weaving on a book

SIMPLICITY

There are so few skills required to make your own frame loom that just about anyone, with any ability or experience level, can make one with time and patience.

A frame loom's simplicity also allows it to be adaptable. If you can't decide whether you want to weave a loose wall hanging with thick roving or a tightly woven bookmark with thin threads and yarns, don't worry; the frame loom can accommodate both. With the nail spacing instructions included later in this chapter, you'll be able to get a wide project variety from a single frame loom. Switching between warping around every nail and warping around every other or every two nails will allow you to use the same loom to weave both loose and dense weavings with ease.

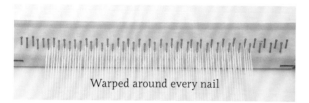

Warped around every nail

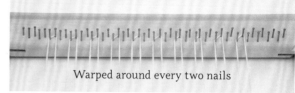

Warped around every two nails

SIZE

Another big benefit of weaving with a frame loom is the loom's size. Generally speaking, the depth of a frame loom doesn't measure more than 1" (2.5cm). This means that you can stack several frame looms on top of one another to store them without taking up a lot of space. The frame loom is an excellent companion for the weaver with limited storage space or the weaver on the go.

Depending on the height and width of your loom, you can take it just about anywhere that you would take a book or a laptop. Whether you're in bed, on the couch, or travelling by car or plane, it can be as discreet and compact as pulling out an embroidery or knitting project.

The design of the frame loom also makes it incredibly convenient for completing projects quickly, unlike other kinds of looms that can take several days to warp alone. You might not be too concerned with this if you're weaving at a leisurely pace for fun, but if you're weaving pieces to sell or share, it can be much more profitable if you're able to complete an entire project in a single day.

Having a few frame looms in a variety of sizes is also extremely valuable. Without the ability to switch sizes, you might end up weaving a small bookmark on a large loom, which is awkward, impractical, and unnecessarily wastes warp fibre. If you get up to weaving at a size that's too large to rest comfortably on your lap, you can build wooden legs or buy a ready-made support stand. With small alterations like these, the sizing possibilities are limitless.

Finally, the size of a frame loom pairs well with physical comfort. If you find yourself weaving for many hours a day like me, you'll want to be aware of your posture and support for your back, shoulders, and neck. Spending long hours doing anything consistently will inevitably cause aches and pains if you're not proactive and conscious of your body's comfort. Knowing your limits is important. I know it's time (or maybe a bit past time) for me to get up, take a break, and stretch when I get a tingly muscle ache in my shoulders. Your body will tell you when it's being overworked. Listen to it!

Parts of the Loom

THE FRAME

The lengths of the bars in the frame can be any dimensions you choose, so long as the two pairs of bars running parallel are the same length as each other. If you use different lengths for each bar or piece of wood, your weavings will end up looking wonky and crooked, just like your frame. But hey, maybe that's an aesthetic choice worth exploring.

NAILS OR PEGS

I recommend using finishing nails on the loom. They're great because they are small, are lightweight, and have very small heads. If you can't find finishing nails, any other thin nails will work.

These nails will act as the anchors for each line of warp fibre. If you're looking to buy a ready-made frame loom, you might come across looms that have pegs or notches in place of nails. I have always preferred using nails because I think they do a better job maintaining tension. Some weavers choose not to use nails, notches, or pegs of any kind and instead prefer to wrap their warp material all the way around the frame. All of these options will produce similar effects, but each one is unique, so you might prefer one to another.

There are many methods and techniques to choose from or develop when it comes to weaving, and I encourage you to explore a few of them so that you know what works best for you.

Building Your Own Frame Loom

CHOOSING A SIZE

The first thing you need to do before heading out to buy materials is to decide how large you want the loom to be.

Where in your home will you want to weave? Where will you store the loom? Will you have to hang it up high on a wall so that your cat won't be able to reach it? These are all good questions to ask yourself. Keep in mind that a larger loom might require a table to rest against, and the larger the loom, the more space your arms will need while actually weaving.

Also think about the project potential of your loom. Do you want to make only bookmarks or coasters right now? Or are you planning on creating pillows and rugs too?

If you've never woven before, I recommend starting on the smaller side, such as 11″ × 14″ (27.9cm × 35.5cm), until you're comfortable with the basics. A good medium size is about 18″ × 18″ (45.7cm × 45.7cm), and a good large frame loom is about 30″ × 30″ (76.2cm × 76.2cm). I find that it's easier to work with a square loom as I'm moving larger, but it's completely up to you.

Keep in mind that whatever measurement you choose for the top and bottom bars, your weaving size will be about four inches smaller in width. This is because you will be weaving only in the center open space of the frame.

Following the instructions for building your own frame loom in this chapter will give you a great starter loom, 11″ × 14″ (27.9cm × 35.5cm), that will be comfortable for small weaving projects from bookmarks to small wall hangings. Three of the projects in this book can be made using this size loom (bookmark, brooch, coaster), and I'll recommend two larger looms for the more advanced projects (pillow, necklace, and both wall hangings).

Supplies

4 canvas stretcher bars

- 2 bars measuring 11″ (27.9cm)
- 2 bars measuring 14″ (35.5cm)

Approximately 60 finishing nails of 1″ (2.5cm)

Measuring tape or ruler with ¼″ (0.6cm) markings

Hammer

Pencil

Towel or blanket

Safety glasses

Frame loom-making supplies

CONSTRUCTING THE FRAME

Whenever you're using a hammer, it's a good idea to wear safety glasses to protect your eyes in case anything flies up toward your face.

STEP 1: Start by laying out the supplies and making sure you have everything you need. The more organized you are, the more enjoyable the process will be.

STEP 2: Lay down a blanket or towel on a hard surface, like a table or the floor. Hammering the bars together on top of the fabric will help keep the bars from slipping and reduce noise.

Hammering bars 1 and 2 together

STEP 3

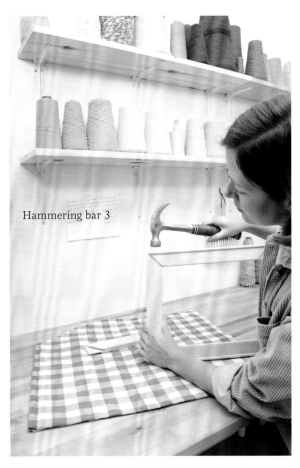

Hammering bar 3

Begin by hammering one 11″ (27.9cm) bar into the corner slot of one 14″ (35.5cm) bar. Then hammer in the remaining two bars to form a rectangular frame.

STEP 4: If the frame looks a bit crooked, keep hammering the corners until they are all the way flush against each other and the frame is level.

MEASURE THE NAIL SPACING

On any given loom in my studio, there might be 100 to 160 nails. I use a lot of nails because I love having a really tight and closely spaced warp for my weavings.

More nails = closer warp spacing = a more dense weave + thinner weft yarn

Fewer nails = wider warp spacing = a looser weave + thicker weft yarn

On this loom, we want to be able to achieve a close warp spacing. So the nails will be ¼" (6mm) apart. Remember that you can always skip nails later on if you want to warp a looser weave.

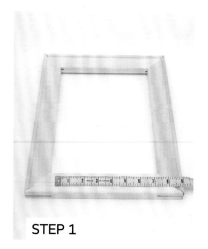

STEP 1

Lay the measuring tape or ruler down on one of the 11" (27.9cm) top or bottom frame bars roughly ½" (1.2cm) away from the inside left edge.

STEP 2

Starting ½" (1.2cm) away from the inner left corner of the frame, make a small dot or line with your pencil at every ¼" (6mm) until you reach ½" (1.2cm) away from the right inner corner of the frame.

Ready for nails

STEP 3

Flip the frame around, and do the same to the opposite bar.

HAMMER IN THE NAILS

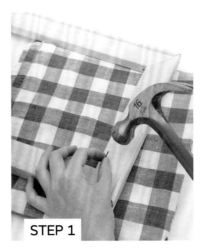

STEP 1

STEP 2

It's best to hammer in the nails with the frame lying on top of a blanket or towel. This will help to absorb the shock of each hit.

We're going to create two staggered rows of nails as opposed to one straight row. Staggering the nails will help prevent the wood from splitting under the pressure.

It's important to hammer the nails in at a slight angle. Hammer the first nail in on the first pencil mark, angling the head of the nail to be leaning back toward the outside of the frame. Angling the nails will ensure that the warp fibre will sit flush against the wood when the loom is warped.

Hammer the second nail into the frame slightly below the first nail, making it closer to the outside of the frame than the first. There's not an exact measurement for the distance between the rows, but they should be between ³⁄₁₆″ (5mm) and ½″ (1.2cm) apart. Make sure both nails are slightly angled toward the outside of the frame.

STEP 3: Hammer the third nail into the frame on the pencil mark, even with the first nail.

STEP 4: Continue this process, following Steps 1-3 until you've reached the end of the bar, then rotate the frame around, and do the same thing on the opposite bar.

You now have your own loom!

Completed frame loom

Photo by Isaac Vallentin

CHAPTER 3
Colour and Design

Colour Theory

Colour theory is, as I'm sure you've guessed, the theory of colour and colour relationships, and it dates back *thousands* of years in some form or another.

Colour has long been thought useful or relevant to the healing of illness and responsible for representing a mood or feeling. We all have feelings toward particular tints, shades, or tones of a colour and often find ourselves gravitating toward the ones that make us feel good for some inexplicable reason. These colour preferences are apparent in everything we do each day, from getting dressed in the morning to reaching for one coffee mug over another to selecting the paint colours that adorn the walls of our homes.

For the past three or four years, my weaving practice has focused primarily on the study of colour relationships. This study is motivated by my fascination with how our perception of colour changes when certain colours are paired together. Put simply, blue next to green has a completely different visual effect and *mood* than does blue next to orange.

My goal with this chapter is not to give you a complete and exhaustive explanation of the history of colour theory and design and what every term means but rather to lay out the basics that will provide some guidance when you're selecting a colour palette and planning the designs of your weaving projects.

A Few Basic Colour Terms

VALUE: Lightness or darkness of a colour defined by how close it is to white or black (A lighter colour has a higher value and more white; a darker colour has a lower value and more black.)

TINT: The lighter value of a colour, created by adding white

SHADE: The darker value of a colour, created by adding black

TONE: The colour that is created when a hue is blended with gray

HUE: A synonym for colour; the purest and brightest form of a colour

COLOUR RELATIONSHIPS

When learning about colour theory, the colour wheel is your best tool.

A basic colour wheel is made up of twelve colours. Three of them are primary (red, blue, yellow), three of them are secondary (green, violet, orange), and the remaining six are tertiary (blue-green, blue-violet, red-orange, red-violet, yellow-orange, yellow-green).

There are some color groupings that are naturally appealing to our eyes:

ANALOGOUS COLOURS are adjacent to each other on the colour wheel. In sets of three, they make a successful palette.

Ex. Yellow-orange, orange, red-orange

COMPLEMENTARY COLOURS sit directly across from each other on the colour wheel. These pairs of colours will always look good together, no matter their tone or shade.

Ex. Blue and orange, purple and yellow, red and green

MONOCHROMATIC COLOURS are tints, tones, and shades of a single hue. These variations are created by respectively adding white, gray, or black to a colour to make them lighter or darker.

Ex. Light purple, midtone purple, dark purple

COLOUR TOOLS

If you aren't confident in selecting a colour palette based on *feeling* alone, or you want to go a step beyond these basic relationships, there are many great colour palette-building tools out there that can remove the guessing and help you put together a pleasing palette really quickly.

A tool that I really love is the *Ultimate 3-in-1 Color Tool* by Joen Wolfrom.

This tool has 24 colour cards with numbered swatches, 5 colour plans for each colour, and two transparent value finders in red and green to help determine value contrasts.

The colour plans outline relationships that work well for a colour, including good matches for tones, shades, and tints as well as the monochromatic, complementary, analogous, split-complementary (variation

Photo by Isaac Vallentin

on complementary), and triadic (sets of three colours that are evenly spaced from each other on the colour wheel) colour relationships.

When using this tool to build a weaving colour palette, select one colour of yarn to start things off. Flip through the 3-in-1 tool to find the hue that is most similar to the yarn, then consult the back of the card to read all of the information about its relationship to other colours.

For example, I want to base a weaving on the blue colour of the yarn in the image above. I found the colour family that looks most like the yarn on card #12, blue-violet. The back of the card shows that its complementary colour is golden yellow and its analogous colours are blue, blue-violet, and violet.

From here, I can pull other colours in the blue-violet monochromatic scheme to create dimension in my weaving as well as a nice bright golden yellow for contrast. You may not be able to find yarn in the exact colours that you want to match a colour family on one of the cards, but that's okay. Think of this tool as a guide, and allow yourself space to explore beyond it.

NATURE AS INSPIRATION

Take a look at the images below.

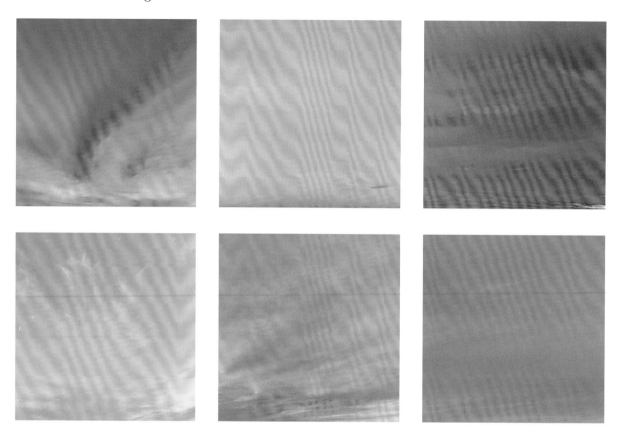

These are all cropped and unedited sunset snapshots taken with an iPhone at my mother's house in the country. Her house is up on a hill with a view of farmers' fields in the back and the ocean in the front. The resulting sunsets over this landscape are magic, often producing colour palettes better than I could ever dream up.

Another way that you might find inspiration is by collecting pieces of litter that you come across while on a walk in your neighbourhood. Challenge yourself to weave something using the colours of the next two pieces you find (while helping clean your community!).

Or at the grocery store you might decide to build a palette with the colours of whatever fruit is on sale that day.

Living in a coastal Nova Scotia town provides so many beautiful opportunities to get inspired by nature in the summer. One of my favourite things to do when I'm at the beach is to look for pieces of washed-up lobster rope. The colours are usually bright, making them easy to spot in the sand. Whenever I find one, it feels like I've found a little treasure.

The point is, inspiration is everywhere.

The key to a good colour palette isn't always that it's perfectly balanced and based on any colour scale or wheel. Choose colours that make you feel good. If you're thoughtful and confident in your selection, they'll be successful.

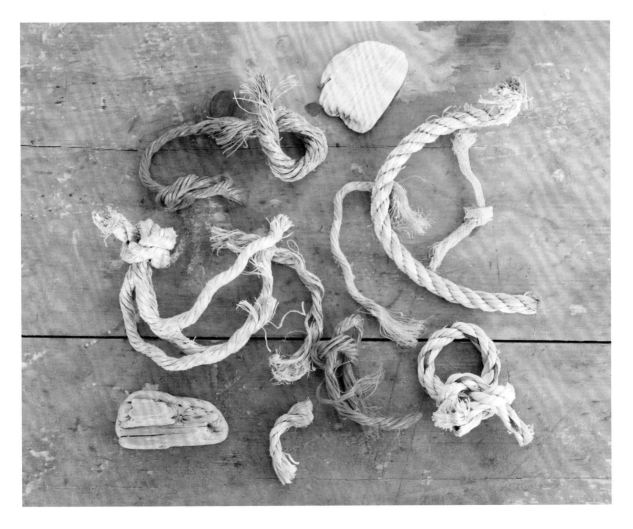

Colour and Design
Weaving Exercises

Here are a couple of fun and easy weaving exercises on paper that are great for quickly testing out your colour ideas. *No loom required!*

WEAVING WITH STRIPS OF PAPER

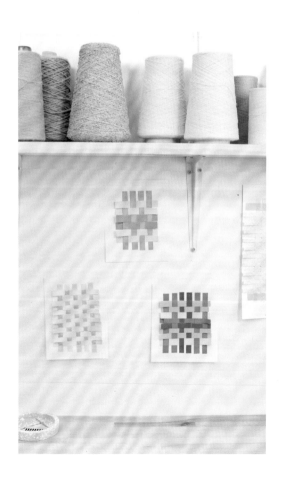

I love this exercise because it's not precious. It's great for easily changing out different colours without worrying about it taking up much of your time. I encourage you to experiment with many colours of paper, both light and dark or bright and dull, to see the different effects that you can create. If you want to remember what a previous version looks like before you swap out the paper strips, snap a photo with your phone to refer to later on.

Tools & Materials
Colourful paper or cardstock

Tape

Scissors for paper

Notes on Exercise Materials
You need coloured paper of any kind. This could be already-coloured construction paper or white paper that you colour or paint using whatever materials you have on hand.

Plain Weave

Please see The Three Basic Weaves on page 54 for images and illustrations of how to weave a plain-woven pattern.

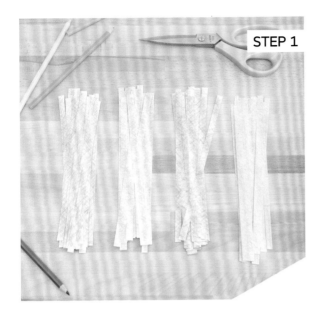

Colour, paint, or purchase several pieces of paper in as many colours as you'd like. If the papers are different sizes, cut them down so that they are all the same width and height. Leave one larger piece of paper uncut for the background.

Stack the papers together, and cut them into thin, long, equally sized strips. These strips don't have to be cut perfectly straight, but feel free to use a straight-edge to mark the strips with a pencil first if you'd like.

Lay down paper strips vertically and evenly spaced on the background piece of paper to create a warp, and then tape them down along the top or bottom, depending on the direction in which you prefer to weave. Tape the background to a hard surface to keep everything in place while you work.

TIP | YOU CAN DO THIS EXERCISE WITHOUT TAPING THE STRIPS TO A BACKGROUND PIECE OF PAPER. JUST LAY THE WARP ON ANY HARD SURFACE, AND USE THE STRIPS TO EXPERIMENT. YOU CAN PULL APART THE WOVEN STRIPS AT THE END AND USE THEM FOR EXPERIMENTATION LATER.

STEP 3

Select a paper strip and begin to plain weave (page 54), weaving it over one, under one, over one, and so forth all the way across using your hands. After completing the first weft row, push it toward the taped edge.

STEP 4

Continue weaving in the paper strips one at a time until all of the warp strips are covered. Remember to gently push each row flush with the previous one as you go. Play around with different colour combinations until you've created something that excites and inspires you.

Tape down the second side of the warp strip ends to keep your weaving intact. Display it on your wall to inspire your next weaving project.

STEP 5

WEAVING WITH YARN ON PAPER

The purpose of this exercise is to play with colour and test out the effects of layering different colours together. I love making these weavings on paper whenever I feel like I'm in a creative rut. They're a quick and satisfying way to learn about colour pairings that you may not have thought about using together otherwise. The options are limitless: Using several colours or frequently alternating between just two will make for a really interesting design. Push your boundaries!

Tools & Materials

Chenille needle

Small weaving comb (optional)

Scissors

5 selected yarns

Paper or cardstock

Notes on Exercise Materials

Since you will be piercing through to the other side of the paper or cardstock, you need to use a weaving needle with a sharp point. This will help to ensure that the paper doesn't rip when you poke the needle through.

You can use any type of yarn for the warp and weft of this paper-weaving exercise, but keep in mind that you want to use a yarn that is about the same thickness as the thickest part of the needle or slightly thinner. This will help to ensure that the needle will create the perfect-sized hole to pull the yarn through. If the needle makes a hole that is too small for the yarn to be pulled through easily, the pressure from the yarn could rip the paper, making it difficult to complete the exercise.

When selecting the paper for this exercise, I recommend using something thicker and stronger than regular printer paper. A 110-pound cardstock is ideal because it is thin enough to puncture with the needle but not so flexible that it will easily rip.

Plain Weave

Please see The Three Basic Weaves on page 54 for images and illustrations of how to weave a plain-woven pattern.

STEP 1

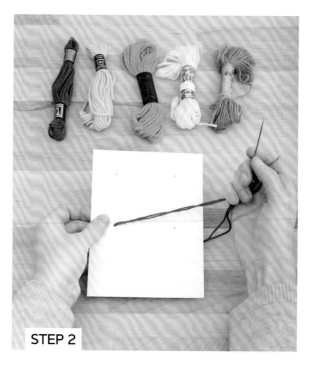

STEP 2

Begin by cutting a piece of cardstock to how-ever large you want the piece to be. Then decide how large you would like the weaving to be on the paper. The paper in my project is 5″ × 6.5″ (12.7cm × 16.5cm), and the weaving is about 3″ × 2.5″ (7.6cm × 6.4cm). Mark the four cor-ners of the area you're going to weave with a small pencil dot or line.

Cut a piece of the first selected yarn about 24″ (61cm) long, fold it in half (for the same look of a thicker strand shown in my project), and thread the chenille needle with it. Hold the piece of paper in one hand, and push the needle through the paper from back to front on the dot in the bottom left corner.

It helps to hold the paper in front of a light to see the needle through the paper.

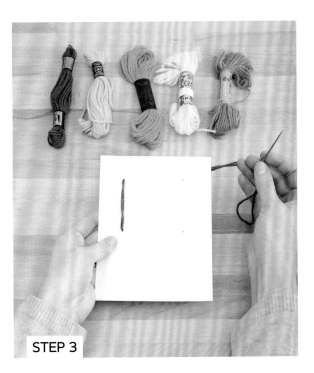

STEP 3

STEP 4

Pull most of the yarn through, leaving a 3″ (7.6cm) long yarn tail on the back. Push the needle from front to back through the marked corner directly above, and pull the yarn all the way through to the back. This is the first warp line.

To keep the paper from bending out of shape, do your best to weave slowly and maintain a consistent and relaxed tension. Don't pull the yarn too tightly at any point.

Push the needle through the paper from back to front about ¼″ (6mm) to the right of the hole you just made. Pull the yarn through, leaving no slack on the back. Then push the needle through from front to back to the right of the first hole on the bottom row, and pull the yarn through. This is the second warp line.

If you want the warp to be more than one colour, switch to a different yarn. You can switch colours for any warp line, but only do so when the needle is on the back side of the paper so that all of the yarn ends will be on the back of the project.

STEP 5

STEP 6

Continue warping the entire marked area, repeating Steps 1-4, and ending on the back side.

Continue using the piece of yarn that is still attached, or choose another colour of yarn and rethread the chenille needle. Push the needle through the paper from back to front slightly above and next to the bottom right corner hole.

Pull the yarn through. If you threaded a new color, leave a 3″ (7.6cm) yarn tail on the back. If you're using the same piece from the warp, pull it flush. It's time to start plain weaving (page 54). Weave over one warp string, under one, over one, under one, all the way across the warp. Then, push the needle through to the back of the paper slightly above and beside the bottom left corner hole. Pull the yarn through.

Poke the needle back through to the front, slightly above where you last went down, and weave back across. Push the needle through to the back of the paper to finish the second weft row.

STEP 7: Continue weaving, stitching through the paper at either end of each weft row, until you've filled the entire warp space. Change yarn colours as often as desired. Optional: Use a comb between each weft row to push the weft together for a tighter weave and to keep the woven lines in place.

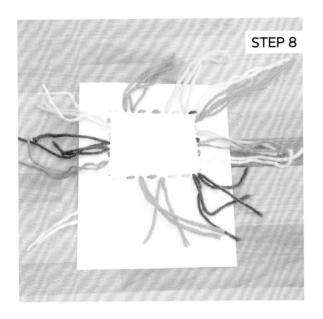

STEP 8

Turn the paper over to secure all of the loose yarn tails. Thread one tail on the needle, and then tuck the tail back and forth through the loops on the back side of the paper. Continue doing this with each tail until they've all been secured. Trim them shorter if you'd like, but not so short that they might pull back through to the front of the paper!

The completed exercise

Elements of Design

There are so many elements of design relevant to different kinds of art, but for weaving purposes, I have included seven big ones: line, shape, colour, texture, space, form, and value.

These elements are used by artists and designers to create successful compositions in their work. There are no true *rules* for what to incorporate in order to create a successful image. Over time, you will develop an instinct for design and be able to make adjustments to all of these elements until you can say, *Ah yes, that's good.*

Designing may come naturally to you, but if it doesn't, or if you *think* it doesn't and are not sure where to start, I suggest focusing on colour first. Try some of the exercises we just went through. Take a moment to lay your yarns out on a table and move them around until you find a placement that you like. Then you can begin to think of how you want to weave the colours together. You can sketch something out or just jump right into it. This whole process is best when it's fun, so do whatever feels right to you.

In addition, consider these elements when you're planning a weaving project.

1. LINES direct the eye where to go, creating movement and flow. A line is any two connected points.

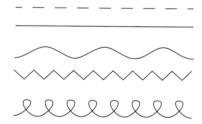

2. SHAPES are two-dimensional enclosed spaces that can be organic or geometric in style.

3. COLOURS are typically what we notice first when we look at something. We've already talked about them quite a bit. Start this chapter over (page 30) for a refresher.

4. TEXTURE provides interest and depth, which is especially true in weaving. When something has an intriguing texture, it draws us closer and makes us want to touch it.

5. SPACE is broken up into positive and negative. Positive space is typically the focal point or the subject, sitting more in the foreground, and the negative space falls behind and becomes a part of the background.

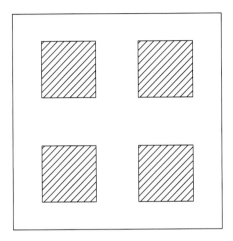

6. FORM has a three-dimensional quality and is created by combining positive space and shape.

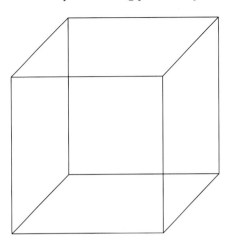

7. VALUE is related to colour but is considered a design element all on its own. Playing around with the lightness and darkness of a colour can add an illusion of mass by creating shadow. In weaving, this is done through gradients by using different values of a single hue.

In general, you may not consider every one of these elements each time you make something, but if a design falls flat, you want to shake things up, or you know you want to elicit a specific effect, these elements are a great place to start when evaluating and making adjustments to your work.

CHAPTER 4
Warping the Loom

Calculations and Planning on a Grid

Before you warp the loom, think about how wide and long you want the weaving to be and if there will be any raised elements or fringe in the middle of the piece.

These considerations will help you to determine what size loom you need and how many warp strings you need to accommodate the width or length of the weaving you want to make.

I find it helpful to think of the warped area as a grid. The frame loom makes it easy to think of your design on × (horizontal) and y (vertical) axes.

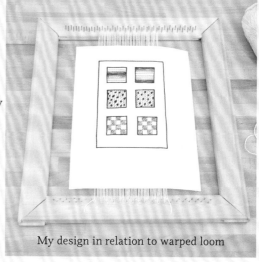
My design in relation to warped loom

Starting with a simple, to-scale sketch of your idea is a great way to make sure you are warping the loom with enough wiggle room. Place your sketch on a table, and lay the loom over or under it to help you visualize where to begin and end your warp. If you know that you want to have raised elements in your weaving, it can be helpful to begin counting warp strings based on those shapes, adding more strings as needed for the flat-woven space around them. See Rya Knots and Raised Elements (page 58) for more information.

TIP | IT'S ALWAYS A GOOD IDEA TO USE AN EVEN NUMBER OF WARP STRINGS. THIS WILL ENSURE THAT YOU WILL BE ABLE TO ADD RYA KNOTS TO YOUR WORK. EACH KNOT NEEDS AN EVEN NUMBER OF WARP STRINGS TO BE INSERTED, SO WITH AN ODD NUMBER OF WARP STRINGS, YOU MAY RUN INTO ISSUES. WE'LL TALK MORE ABOUT RYA KNOTS LATER (PAGE 58).

SPACE CALCULATION EXAMPLE

I have decided that I want to have four raised squares in my weaving, and I want each square to measure 1¼" (3.2cm) wide. I want there to be a 1" (2.5cm) border around all of the squares.

By measuring on the loom, I know that 1" of warped space on my loom is about eleven warp strings when I've warped around every nail.

Since I want the squares to measure 1¼" (3.2cm) wide and they'll need an even number of warp strings, I know that they'll need fourteen warp strings because twelve will be too few and thirteen is an odd number.

I want the space between the squares to measure a little more than half as wide as the border on the edges, so I'll need six warp strings in the middle.

So when considering all four squares in the design, the total number of warp strings needed to execute this design is 56 (on a frame loom that has 11 warp strings per inch).

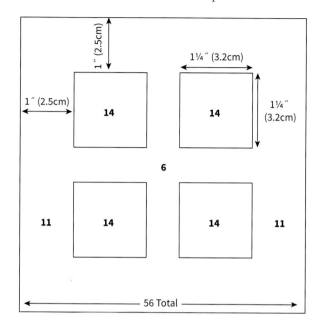

TIP | WARPING THE LOOM WITH THE CORRECT TENSION IS POSSIBLY THE MOST IMPORTANT THING TO DO BEFORE YOU START WEAVING.

IF THE WARP TENSION IS TOO LOOSE, YOU WILL HAVE DIFFICULTY MAINTAINING CONTROL OVER YOUR DESIGN, SENDING THE WHOLE WEAVING OUT OF BALANCE. IT ISN'T REALLY POSSIBLE TO WARP THE LOOM TOO TIGHTLY, UNLESS THE STRING BREAKS AS YOU'RE PULLING IT. SO YOU WANT TO PULL THE WARP STRING AS TIGHTLY AS THE MATERIAL WILL ALLOW, WITHOUT CAUSING IT TO SNAP UNDER EXCESSIVE PRESSURE.

How to Warp a Frame Loom

STEP 1

Pull out the end of the warp string, and keep it attached to its ball, skein, or cone. Tie a knot around the first nail needed for your design on the bottom row. Double knot it to be sure it won't budge.

Incorrect

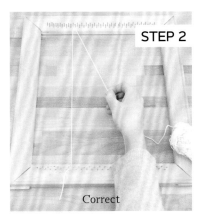

Correct

Pull the warp string up from the nail it's tied to, and wrap it around the nail directly across at the top of the loom. If you're not sure which nail to wrap around, look at the open space created between the edge of the frame and the warp string. Is the space even at the top and bottom?

You want the lines to be parallel; otherwise the weaving will be crooked.

STEP 3

Keeping warp evenly taut by placing my finger on string at bottom of loom

STEP 4

STEP 5

Once you've wrapped the string around the first nail at the top, bring it down and wrap it around the second nail on the bottom. Pull and wrap it with as much tension and tightness as you can without breaking the string. You want the string to be pulled perfectly taut.

Continue wrapping the string around each nail on the top and bottom all the way across the desired width of the weaving-to-be. Make sure that you are holding the tension of the previous string in place as you wrap around the next nail.

Tie the warp string end around the last nail at the bottom, holding the tension in place until that knot is doubled and secured.

When the warp is in place, you should be able to bounce your hand on it without any strings sinking lower than others.

TIP | IF YOU NOTICE THAT YOU'VE ACCIDENTALLY SKIPPED A NAIL OR TWO, OR THAT ONE AREA HAS LOOSER TENSION THAN THE REST, IT'S ALWAYS BEST TO START THE WARP OVER AGAIN. IT'S IMPORTANT THAT THE WARP IS CONSISTENT THROUGHOUT ITS WIDTH.

SOMETIMES WHEN I'M HALFWAY THROUGH WARPING THE LOOM, I'LL COME ACROSS A KNOT IN THE BALL OR SKEIN OF YARN I'M USING. THIS IS ANOTHER GOOD EXAMPLE OF WHEN YOU MAY NEED TO RESTART THE WARP FROM THE BEGINNING.

CHAPTER 5

Starting to Weave

Where to Start

There is no rule for the direction in which you weave on the loom. You can weave from the top of the loom down or from the bottom of the loom up; it doesn't matter. Some weavers even weave with their design upside down and backwards on the loom. It's all up to you and your preference.

I've always woven from the top of the loom down because I like to use the leftover warp strings at the bottom of my weaving as fringe, and I find that weaving in this direction works best for that.

Photo by Isaac Vallentin

Tension of the Weft

Just like the tension of the warp, the tension of the weft is very important. The tension of the weft is what controls the straightness of the vertical edges of each weaving (also called *selvedges*). It also controls the consistency in the weft lines.

Maintaining consistently good tension throughout your weaving—not too tight and not too loose—is essential to creating a balanced weave and is how you avoid the dreaded hourglass effect.

When you pull too tightly on each woven line, the two selvedges will gradually taper inward, creating what looks like an hourglass shape. When you notice this happening, it's already too late to fix as you continue. The best solution is to pull out the last few woven lines where they start to taper and try again, focusing on maintaining even tension.

Hourglass effect

Photo by Isaac Vallentin

STRAIGHT SELVEDGES

There are a few things that you can do to practice perfecting your weft tension.

Bubbles

One trick is to create bubbles on each woven line before combing it. To create bubbles, weave a loose wavy line across the warp. Then push the line up to the previous woven line at a few evenly spaced points with the weaving needle.

This can help to train your hand not to pull too tightly as you're weaving across the warp. One disclaimer: I find it tricky to use the bubble technique on a warp with eleven strings per inch because the bubbles don't slide into place easily on a dense warp.

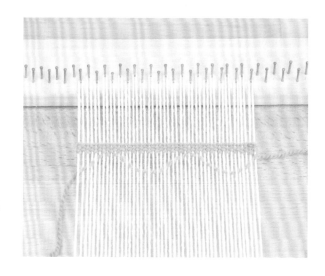

Setting the Weft Line at the Edge First

Another useful trick is to set the edge of the weft line. To do this, weave a line, but don't comb it. Then, pull out the warp string on the furthest outer edge, and push the weft yarn up with the needle in your other hand. This will help to ensure that the edge of the weaving stays consistent with each line as you're weaving.

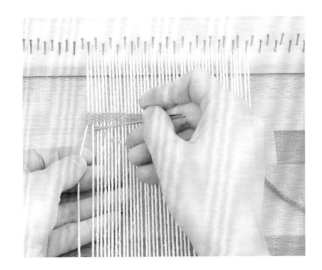

Turn the Loom Upside Down

The best way to check if the edges are straight and parallel is simply to turn the loom 180°, until it is upside down. The corners of the frame loom can sometimes shift and become crooked with lots of use, causing you to weave on a subtle diagonal. Turning the loom upside down will show you if you need to readjust the frame or your weaving angle moving forward.

When I discovered this trick, I was surprised by how much my eyes deceive me by showing me what I want to see rather than what's actually in front of me.

What it should look like when you turn loom upside down: selvedges straight and weft section parallel to frame

TIP | ANOTHER GREAT EXERCISE FOR TENSION IS TO PRACTICE WEAVING WITH A VARIETY OF YARN WEIGHTS AND TEXTURES WHILE STICKING WITH ONE CONSISTENT WARP YARN. YOUR TENSION WILL IMPROVE WITH PRACTICE AS YOU GET TO KNOW HOW THE DIFFERENT WEFT YARNS REACT TO THE SAME WARP YARN.

Combing the Weft

Depending on the density of your weaving, you may need to comb the weft after each line is woven. The denser the weaving, the more often you will need to comb the weft lines. The more you weave, the more combing will become an intuitive motion for you.

To comb up the weft, simply insert a comb between the warp strings and push up with your hand until the newest weft line is flush with the previous one. I like to alternate between combing up with my comb and using my weaving needle to push up my weft after each woven line. If you're weaving from bottom to top, you can do the same motion in the opposite direction.

The Three Basic Weaves

PLAIN WEAVE

A plain weave is sometimes called a tabby weave. It's the most basic type of weave. Weave the weft yarn over one warp string, under one warp string, over, under, all the way across.

Sometimes weaving patterns use a ratio notation to indicate how you should weave. For example, "1/1" indicates one weave over the warp to one weave under the warp, which is a plain weave. This notation can help you remember the weaving pattern in a simple way.

How plain weave is indicated graphically on weaving pattern: Each column of squares represents one warp string, each row represents one weft line. Dark square indicates weaving over warp, light square indicates weaving under warp.

1/1 plain weave

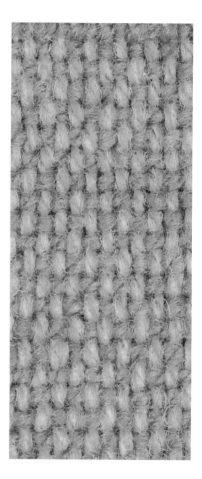

TWILL WEAVE

A twill weave is created when you weave over at least *one* warp string, then under at least *two* warp strings to create a pattern of diagonal lines. So a twill weave might look a variety of ways: 1/2, 2/2, 2/4, and so forth. For the twill design to be successful, you must keep whatever pattern you choose consistent with each weft line.

Here is an example of a 2/2 twill weave pattern where two warp strings are woven over, then two are woven under for the entire weave.

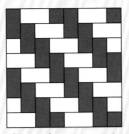

Graphic/grid representation of twill weave. Each column of squares represents one warp string, each row represents one weft line. Dark squares indicate weaving over warp, light squares indicate weaving under warp. Rectangles represent two squares.

2/2 twill weave

2/2 twill weave with alternating sections of yellow and light gray warp and weft.

SATIN WEAVE

A satin weave is achieved by either weaving under at least four warp strings and then over one, *or* weaving over at least four warp strings and under one. So a 1/4 or 4/1 pattern.

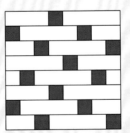

Graphic/grid representation of satin weave. Each column of squares represents one warp string, each row represents one weft line. Dark square indicates weaving over warp, light squares indicate weaving under warp. Rectangles represent multiple squares.

1/4 satin weave

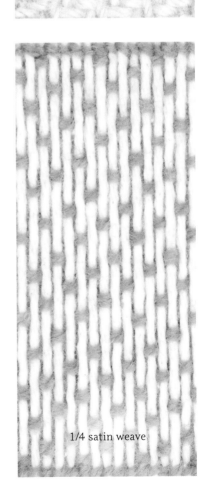

1/4 satin weave

Twining

I call the first line of my weavings a *starting line*. No matter what I'm making or what the piece will look like, I always use a technique called *twining* for my starting line. Whenever I am talking about a starting or finishing line in this book, I am referring to the twining technique.

To start the twining technique, weave a plain-woven line all the way across the warp space. Then, while weaving back in the opposite direction, wrap the needle around the first woven line, still going over and under each warp string.

This ensures that the weaving will not unravel when you cut it off the loom, and it's an elegant way to create a nice clean edge along the top and bottom of a weaving.

A *finishing line* is the exact same technique as the starting line, but it's done at the bottom of the weaving as the last woven line. This technique is especially useful at the bottom of the weaving if you'd like to use the leftover warp strings as your fringe because it ensures that the woven part stays put. You can easily practice twining before starting a project since it's just two quick rows.

TIP | I FIND IT'S EASIER TO WEAVE A FINISHING LINE BY CUTTING A NEW PIECE OF YARN LENGTH (A FEW INCHES MORE THAN DOUBLE THE WIDTH OF THE WEAVING) THAN BY USING THE LEFTOVER WEFT YARN THAT IS STILL ATTACHED AT THE BOTTOM OF THE WEAVING. USING A STAND-ALONE PIECE OF YARN WILL ALLOW YOU TO PULL THE SECOND LINE IN THIS TECHNIQUE FLUSH AND EVEN WITHOUT WORRYING ABOUT HOW THE TENSION OF THIS LINE WILL AFFECT THE LAST WOVEN LINE OF THE WEAVING.

Weft-Joining Techniques

Weft-joining techniques are used to connect two or more separate and adjacent sections of weft or to change the edges of a shape—to turn a square into a circle, for example.

INTERLOCKING

Interlocking is great for connecting two sections without leaving a noticeable seam. This technique can be tricky to do on a densely woven weft. So it's a great option for connecting different sections of loosely woven weft in wall hangings, pillows, or rugs.

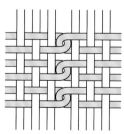

To interlock, one of the two sections you are joining must be already complete (Section A). Then, as you start weaving the second section (Section B), each time you finish a weft line next to Section A, tuck the needle through the loop created by two weft lines of Section A. This will create a chain-like connection between the outermost warp strings of both sections.

DOVETAILING

The dovetailing technique creates a bumpy ridge along the seam where the sections are connected and works really well when connecting densely woven areas.

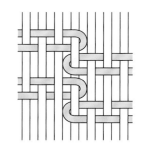

To use this technique, one of the two sections you are joining must be already complete (Section A). Then, as you start weaving the second section (Section B), weave each weft line in between each pair of weft lines in Section A. So Section A and Section B share one warp string.

This is my preferred joining technique for most projects. I use it in a number of ways in my work, most commonly when I am connecting two colours of weft together and when I am turning open warp squares and rectangles into circles and ovals in preparation for rya knots (more on that later; see page 122).

DIAGONAL

The diagonal joining technique is similar to dovetailing, but it's used only when you want to connect or create sections that are curved or triangular. This is the technique that you would use if you wanted to weave a flat-woven circle or triangle into a design.

First, create a plan for the shape you want to weave. Then, weave Section A (weft lines on the left) by weaving on one fewer warp string with each row. This creates a diagonal line. Then, weave Section B (weft lines on the right) by weaving on one additional warp string with each row. Repeat this process as needed to create all sides of the shape. Once combed together, all these lines will be seamlessly connected, and you will have a curved or triangular shape in the weaving (depending on which one you're creating).

SLIT

The slit technique creates an open gap between two warp strings, leaving two weft sections unconnected.

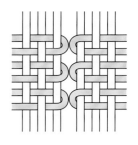

This technique is great for creating a very straight vertical edge in the design. If you want a straight edge but don't want the slit to be open, you can then sew it closed on the back of the weaving with transparent thread after it's taken off the loom. To create a slit, leave two adjacent sections of weft completely unconnected.

I use this technique a lot in flat-woven colour-gradient weavings.

CHAPTER 6
Rya Knots and Raised Elements

A rya knot is a weaving technique that is most commonly used to create fringe at the bottom of a weaving. It's known to create depth and texture.

How to Make a Rya Knot

To create a rya knot, you need two warp strings and a stand-alone piece of yarn at least 3" (2.8cm) long. The knot is created by folding the yarn in half between warp strings. So if you want to have a fringe that measures 6" (5.5cm) long, you will need a piece of yarn that measures double that length. I like to cut a bunch of pieces to the length I need before I start tying the knots. This knot can be created with a weaving needle or your fingers.

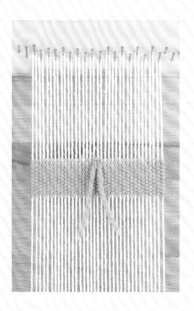

STEP 1: Wrap one end of the yarn over and around the left warp string, bringing it toward the middle of the two warp strings.

STEP 2: Wrap the other side of the yarn over and around the right warp string. Both tails should be coming through the middle of the two warp strings.

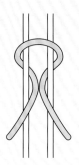

STEP 3: Pull both strings even and tight. That's it!

TIP | WHEN STACKING RYA KNOTS ON TOP OF ONE ANOTHER, YOU WANT THEM TO BE AS CLOSE TO EACH OTHER AS POSSIBLE TO MAKE A DENSE SHAPE.

Stacked rya knots

WHEN YOU HAVE A ROW OF RYA KNOTS, BE CAREFUL NOT TO PULL THE KNOTS SO TIGHTLY THAT THE WARP STRINGS ARE DISTORTED. KNOTS SHOULD BE CLOSE AND TOUCHING BUT NOT SQUEEZED INTO PLACE.

Touching rya knots

Using Rya Knots to Make Fringe

You can add fringe anywhere on a weaving using the same basic rya knot. When using this technique, consider the following:

- To create a thicker fringe, use two or more pieces of yarn to create each rya knot.

- When adding fringe to the bottom of a weaving, weave a few plain-woven lines underneath the line of fringe knots. End with a finishing line to secure them.

- Once the weaving is cut off the loom, tie the warp strings underneath the fringe into knots and trim them short so they'll be hidden. We'll talk more about cutting a weaving off the loom on page 71.

Using Rya Knots to Make 3D Shapes

When creating a raised shape within a weaving, I find it's easiest to first weave the entire surrounding flat-woven area or background. It seems to help with the overall tension of the shape once it's trimmed and the weaving is cut off the loom.

As a general rule, to maximize the density of the knots, it's best to use only one to three strands of yarn per knot, depending on the yarn's thickness. But if you are using a thin yarn to create your knots, you should use as many strands as will make it about the same thickness as, or a bit thicker than, the warp yarn. This will ensure that each knot fills in the right amount of space. To ensure there is enough yarn to trim the shapes after they are attached, I recommend using pieces of yarn for each knot that are at least 3″ (7.6cm) long.

After preparing the background of the weaving and selecting yarn type and length, fill the open warp space on the loom with rya knots. Remember that to make a dense shape, you want the knots to be as close to each other as possible.

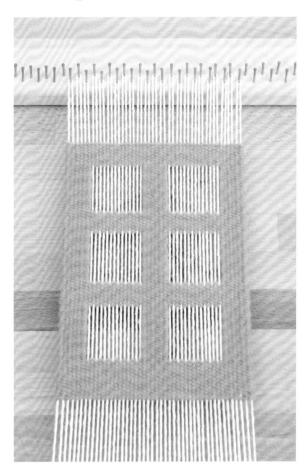

SECURING 3D SHAPES

The most important step in creating raised elements of any shape or pattern is securing them on the back of the weaving before you trim them. This is crucial to controlling and securing the tension of the edges of the weaving and to make sure that the knots are not going to fall out on the front.

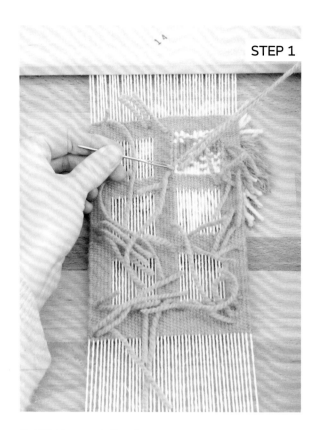

STEP 1

To secure the knots, turn the loom over to the back side. We need to connect one warp string of the rya knot section to the warp string of the flat-woven section to which it is adjacent. Thread a needle with a piece of yarn that matches the flat-woven section. You can use a regular weaving needle for this, but the pointed tip of a chenille needle might make it easier. Sew a whip stitch around the first warp string with knots, starting at the bottom of the left side, going through to the front, and then going back around the outermost warp string of the flat-woven section.

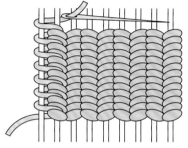

Continue doing this all the way up one side of the knotted shape.

STEP 2: Carefully plain weave across the top of the shape by going over and under every warp string through the knots, and repeat Step 1 to connect the right side of the knot section with the adjacent flat-woven section, moving from top to bottom this time.

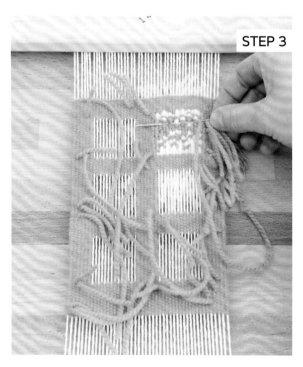

STEP 3

Carefully plain weave a few lines back and forth across the back of the knot section. Make sure to wrap the needle around the innermost warp string of the flat-woven area on both sides of the shape as you move from one woven line to another. Doing this will enable you to tug on this woven line to pull in the edges of the weaving if the tension needs to be corrected along the selvedges.

STEP 4: Cut the yarn, leaving a 2″ (5.1cm) (or longer) tail. Secure the woven lines and stitches you just made by knotting the yarn ends together along edges of the squares. Weave tails into the back of the flat-woven section. See how to weave in yarn ends on page 70.

Now you're ready to trim the shape and reveal the pattern beneath the wild tuft of yarn!

TRIMMING

Trimming the raised elements is my favourite part of the process. I love discovering the colours and patterns that appear as I'm trimming. It's always a surprise, and I always find myself learning something new about colours and their relationships to each other.

There are no rules about trimming rya knots except that it's best to use sharp scissors and to cut less than you think you need to. You can always trim more, but you can't add length back in without starting over.

 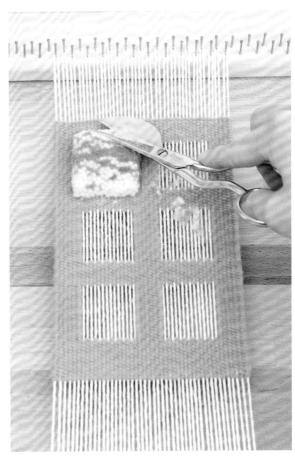

TIP | I LOVE TO SAVE AND MIX MY SCRAPS AFTER TRIMMING. IT HELPS ME DISCOVER NEW COLOR COMBINATIONS, AND THE SCRAPS CAN BE REPURPOSED AS CONFETTI OR STUFFING IN OTHER FUN PROJECTS.

Rya Knot Patterns

Now that you know how to form 3D shapes, it's time to think about how the shapes look. There are lots of pattern techniques you can use to make your shapes look interesting. I'm going to demonstrate these techniques using the 1¼″ (3.2cm) square design we planned out earlier (page 48). But you can practice on any other shape, using at least four sets of two warp strings.

COLOUR GRADIENTS

Let's fill the first square with a colour gradient. To create a raised two-colour gradient, select two colours of yarn, and cut them into 3″ (2.8cm) long pieces. I am using eight to ten strands of a very thin purple yarn per knot, and two strands of white yarn per knot. This ratio will ensure that the two colours occupy the same amount of space once they're trimmed down later on, since the two yarns are different thicknesses.

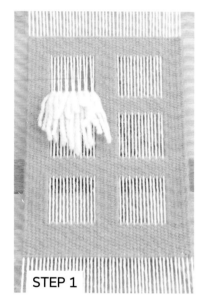

STEP 1

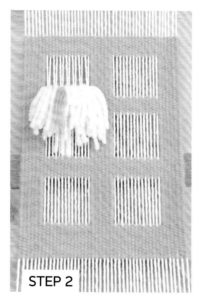

STEP 2

STEP 3

Beginning with the first selected yarn colour, insert one full line of knots along the bottom of the square. For small spaces like these squares, I use a weaving needle to make each knot.

On the second row, add one knot of the second selected yarn colour anywhere in the row to replace one knot of the first colour.

On the third row, add two knots of the second yarn colour anywhere in the row to replace two knots of the first colour.

STEP 4: Continue replacing knots in this gradual pattern with each row until you have one full row of the second yarn colour.

Finished colour gradient,
not trimmed

STEP 5

Trimmed!

Reverse this process, adding in a knot of the first colour in each row, continuing the gradient in the opposite direction. If you run out of space in the shape before completely finishing the gradient, that's fine!

SPECKLES

To create a raised speckled shape, use two or three different-coloured pieces of yarn per knot depending on their thicknesses. If you're using three colours, I recommend using thinner yarns (close to the thickness of your warp yarn or a bit thinner).

Fill the entire shape using a varied number of colours per knot. Play around with the design by using different combinations. The possibilities are endless!

Speckles in progress

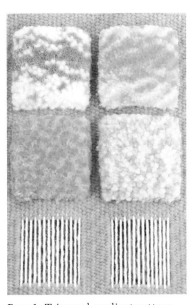

Row 1: Trimmed gradient pattern

Row 2: Trimmed speckled pattern with regular distribution of two colours

CHECKERBOARD

To create a raised checkerboard pattern, use at least two colours of yarn for the knots. Note that each square in the checkerboard pattern is four warp strings wide. So the warp space should be a multiple of four to make sure each square is the same size.

STEP 1

Tie two rya knots with the first chosen yarn colour in Row 1.

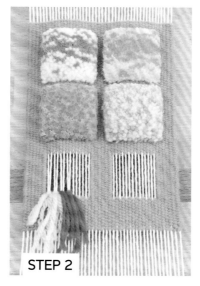

STEP 2

Tie two knots using the second yarn colour in Row 1, next to the first two knots.

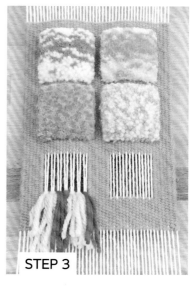

STEP 3

Repeat Steps 1-2 until Row 1 is complete.

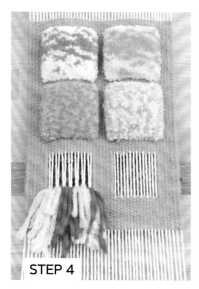

STEP 4

Repeat this colour pattern for the second row of knots.

STEP 5

For the third row, reverse the order of colours so that it begins with the second yarn colour instead of the first.

STEP 6

Repeat this reversed colour pattern for the fourth row of knots.

Row 3: Trimmed checkerboard pattern

STEP 7

Repeat Steps 1-6 until you have filled in the warp space.

TIP | YOU CAN EASILY CREATE A STRIPED PATTERN WITH RYA KNOTS. CHOOSE AT LEAST TWO YARN COLOURS, AND ALTERNATE USING THEM FOR EACH ROW OR COLUMN.

CHAPTER 7
Finishing Techniques

These finishing techniques are what I use most often to finish my work and what I've found to be best suited to small-scale weavings made on a frame loom with eleven warp strings per 1" (2.5cm), which is what we built together earlier (see Chapter 2: The Frame Loom, page 20).

Securing Yarn Ends

There are a few ways to secure loose yarn ends on the back of a weaving.

The first, and most ideal, is to weave the ends into the back of the weaving, hiding them from sight on both sides of the piece. This technique is best for weavings such as coasters, bookmarks, jewelry, and rugs, which are all items that could be handled and viewed from both sides.

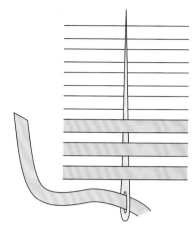

To do this, thread the weaving needle with a yarn end, and then tuck the needle underneath at least three lines of weft either above or below the yarn end. Pull the needle through, and then trim the piece of yarn flush to the weaving. If the yarn end is too short to thread the needle with before tucking in the ends, tuck the needle under the weft first, and then thread the needle right before you pull it through.

If the weaving is very dense, you may not be able to weave the yarn ends in. The next best way to secure them is to tie them in knots. This will create little knot bumps on the back of the project, but they won't be visible on the front.

To tie yarn ends together, use two ends that are right next to each other, and tie them together in a double knot. Trim the excess yarn close to the knot.

This technique is ideal for wall hangings because the back of the weaving will be hidden and not handled on a daily basis.

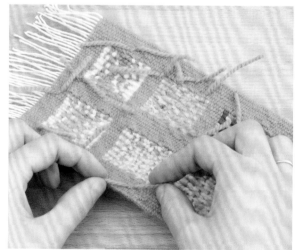

Cutting the Weaving off the Loom

You always want to cut the weaving off as close to the edge of the frame loom as possible. If you're cutting the warp strings close to the weaving, this will make it difficult for you to secure the bottom against unraveling.

This also will give you as much room as possible for using the warp strings as fringe, deciding on the length of the fringe, or tying the warp strings in knots under added rya fringe.

For this reason, it's a good idea to plan to use a loom that is long enough to accommodate a good 4″ (10.2cm) of extra warp space at the bottom of a weaving.

What you do with the top strings will depend on how you want to finish the project. For now, just slip it off the loom. You should have dangling warp strings on the bottom and warp loops along the top.

Cut all the way through bottom warp strings as close to loom as possible.

Attaching a Wooden Dowel and Finishing

There are several methods for handling the loose warp strings and adding strings and dowels for hanging. When planning a weaving, make sure to leave at least 2″ (5.1cm) of warp space at the top for Techniques 2 and 3 below.

TECHNIQUE 1: WOODEN DOWEL AND WARP LOOPS

The easiest way to attach a dowel is to slip the dowel through the warp loops at the top of the finished weaving after you cut it off of the loom. Make sure that the dowel is at least ½″ (1.2cm) longer than the width of the weaving to keep the loops from sliding off the dowel ends. If you are attaching a string for hanging, this string should help prevent the loops from sliding off as well.

TIP | IF YOU ARE PLANNING TO ADD A DOWEL THROUGH THE LOOPS CREATED BY THE LEFTOVER WARP STRINGS AT THE TOP OF A WEAVING, BE SURE THAT THE WARP ENDS ARE BOTH TIED TO THE NAILS ON THE BOTTOM OF THE FRAME SO THAT THE LOOPS WILL BE CREATED ONCE THE WEAVING IS CUT OFF THE LOOM.

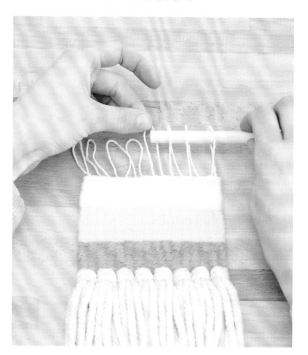

TECHNIQUE 2: TUCKING IN WARP STRINGS

Depending on the loom, you may have warp loops that are uneven in length, which will be obvious and might steal focus from the finished weaving. In the case of uneven loops, it's best to tuck the warp strings into the back of the weaving so that you have a straight and clean woven edge at the top.

To do this, cut the loops into separate strings. Then thread a chenille or weaving needle with each loose warp thread, one at a time, and tuck it through at least three weft lines on the back of the weaving. Pull the tail ends until the warp loops are no longer visible from the front, but don't pull hard enough to curl the top of the weaving.

You can do the same with the bottom warp strings if you don't want to use them for fringe or if you don't have added fringe to knot them behind. If you want to make a project without a dowel attached at the top or fringe hanging at the bottom, you can simply weave all of the warp string ends into the back of the weaving.

TECHNIQUE 3: ATTACHING A DOWEL WITH EXTRA STRING

After tucking in the warp strings, choose a yarn for attaching the dowel. Lay the dowel along the top edge of the weaving, then thread a chenille needle. Next, sew through the top of the weaving and around the dowel, as many times as you'd like. You can do this all the way across the weaving, just on either end and in the middle, or just a few times on each end.

All the way across

Just on ends

Both ends and middle

ATTACHING HANGING STRING TO A DOWEL

Attaching a string for hanging isn't always necessary. You could easily hang a wall hanging by resting the dowel on a few evenly spaced nails. But I always attach strings for hanging my work because my weavings are relatively small scale, and I find that the hanging string helps to visually balance out the fringe at the bottom of the weaving.

Cut a piece of string to your desired length. Tie each end of the string to each end of the dowel, securing each side with a double knot on the back of the dowel.

Superglue

Superglue is an optional tool that can sometimes come in handy for securing slippery yarn ends that are too short to weave in or tie off. It can also provide a quick fix for attaching longer warp string loops to a wooden dowel. While handy in a pinch, superglue should always be used as a last resort (because the glue may degrade the fibres over time) or to provide a solution to a problem that would otherwise cause you to restart your whole project. You can use it to reattach a severed warp string, for example, if you accidentally cut it while you're weaving.

Hand Sewing

If you are weaving a project that requires you to attach several woven pieces together (like the pillow project on page 106), there are two simple hand-sewing techniques that will be handy to know for finishing the project.

RUNNING STITCH

This stitch is one of the most basic and is often used for sewing things together inside out so the stitches will be hidden once the project is turned right side out.

To sew a running stitch, start by threading a chenille needle with thread or yarn. Choosing a yarn that matches your project will help it blend in. Align the two pieces you are sewing together. Tie a knot at the end of the yarn, and while holding the project in your nondominant hand, push the needle up from the bottom through both layers to the top, about ¼"-½" (6mm-1.2cm) away from the edge of what you're sewing. Pull the needle away from the project until the knot is flush with the bottom layer. Complete the first stitch by pushing the needle back through both layers and pulling the stitch flat and flush. Repeat as needed, and end your last stitch with the needle on the back, securing the thread with another knot.

The length of your stitches and the open spaces in between depends on your project and how securely you want these two pieces of material to be attached. The closer they are, the more secure the stitches will be.

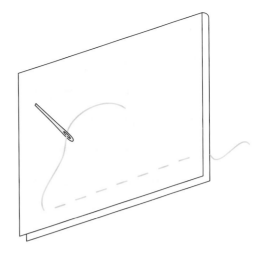

LADDER STITCH

Also known as the invisible stitch, this stitch is ideal for when you want to sew a seam closed on the right side of a project. An example of this would be sewing the pillow project closed after it has been stuffed.

To sew a ladder stitch, thread a chenille needle with matching thread or yarn. Tie a knot at one end of the yarn, and prepare the two pieces that are going to be sewn together. While holding the project in your nondominant hand, push the needle up from the back side of the material about ¼"–½" (6mm–1.2cm) away from the edge or in line with the existing seam if there is one (Step A on the illustration).

Pull the needle away from the material until the knot is flush with the back, and then push the needle through the material on the opposite side of the gap, directly across from where the thread is sticking out (Step B on the illustration). Pull the stitch tight, and then push the needle up through to the front on the same side of the gap, a little bit over from the previous stitch (Step C on the illustration). Repeat as needed (D-J in the illustration), and end the last stitch going through the inside of the project, secured with a knot.

Just like the running stitch, the length of your stitches and the open spaces in between depends on your project and how securely you want these two pieces of material to be attached. The closer the stitches are, the more secure they will be.

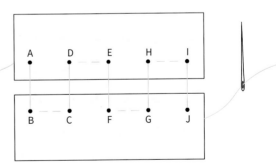

Projects for the Frame Loom

Reminders for Planning a Weaving

- Think about the size of the project, and use a loom that allows for a bit of extra warp space on all sides.

- Choose an appropriate warp yarn for your project (thinner for things like brooches and necklaces, thicker for things like rugs and pillows), and be sure that it is rigid and has zero stretch when pulled.

- Think about your design, and figure out if you need an odd or even number of warp strings. You need an even number for rya knots.

- Don't be afraid to edit your design or colour palette as you're weaving; just be careful not to cut any warp strings if you cut out any sections of weft.

- Double-check that you've woven a finishing line and that everything in the design is complete before cutting the weaving off the loom. Once it's off, it can't go back on!

- Cut the weaving off the loom as close to the frame as possible to allow for some wiggle room for how you want to finish the weaving.

- Always try to weave the yarn ends in on the back of your weaving before trying other methods (tying knots, using superglue).

- Don't forget to have fun and keep practicing!

Woven Bookmark

Tools & Materials

Weaving needle

Measuring tape

Comb

Scissors

8/8-width cotton warp yarn with no stretch

Selected thin weft yarns (about 1mm thick) in 5 colours

Small frame loom, recommended 11" × 14" (27.9cm × 35.5cm)

Superglue (optional)

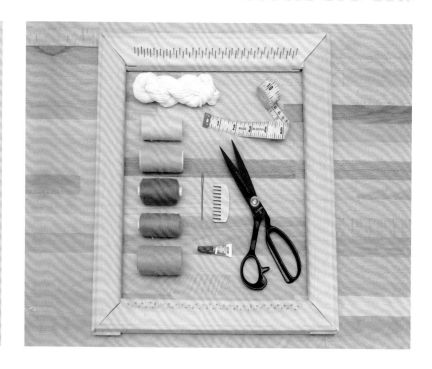

Notes on Project Materials

For the warp of this project, I'm using 8/8 unmercerized brassard cotton weaving yarn from Gist Yarn. This is a great yarn for warping because it has zero stretch, and its thickness helps to create a strong and sturdy bookmark that stands up straight when you hold it. Using a thinner warp yarn will make for a floppier bookmark.

Similar and suitable warp alternatives:

• Bernat Handicrafter cotton yarn

• Lily Sugar 'n Cream Big Ball solids yarn

To keep your bookmark as thin as possible (to allow the pages of your book to close on it), I recommend choosing five weft yarns that are all very similar in weight/thickness to each other and to the warp yarn.

The weft yarns that I'm using are thin vintage wool spools, so I'm using four strands of this fibre where I would normally use one with a heavier-weight yarn.

Techniques Needed for This Project

TWINING, page 56

PLAIN WEAVING, page 54

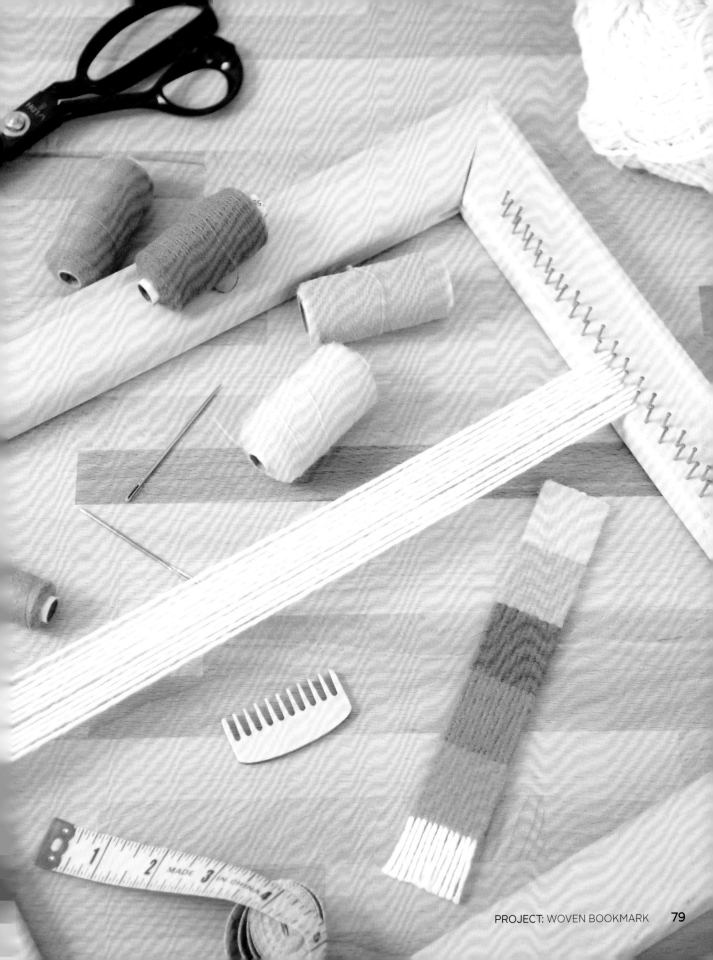

Weaving the Bookmark

The final woven bookmark will measure approximately 1¼" wide × 7¼" long (3.2cm × 18.4cm), including the fringe.

STEP 1

Based on the above measurements, warp the loom with eleven or twelve warp strings for a space measuring 1¼" (3.2cm) wide, approximately six nails at the top of the frame. This measurement doesn't have to be exact.

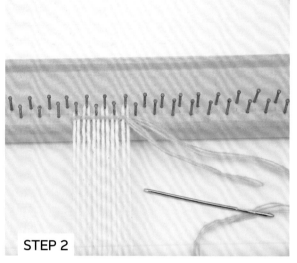

STEP 2

Using a long piece of the first selected weft yarn, weave a starting line at the top of the warped loom, and push it up to the lowest line of nails using the comb.

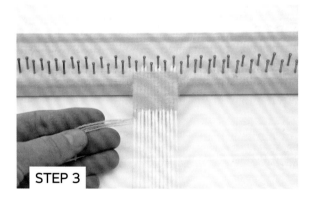

STEP 3

Begin plain weaving (1/1) until the woven section reaches about 1¼" (3.2cm) in length. Then slide the end of the yarn toward the back of the weaving on the left or right side so the tail sticks out toward the back side of the weaving.

Be sure to firmly comb up against the woven lines often as you weave. This will help to create a dense and sturdy bookmark.

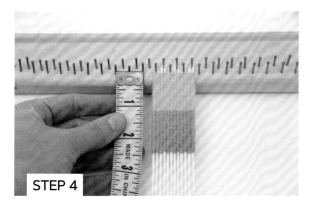

STEP 4

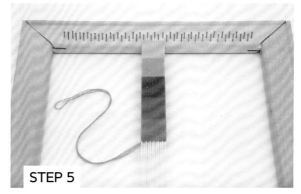

STEP 5

Choose the second selected weft yarn, and weave directly underneath what you've already woven. Continue weaving this second colour, combing up often, until the second woven colour reaches 1¼" (3.2cm) in length. Slide the tail through so it sticks out on the back of the weaving.

Repeat Step 4 for the three remaining selected weft yarns.

Now that you've woven in all five colours, the bookmark should measure about 6½" (16.5cm) long.

STEP 6: Weave a finishing line in the same colour as the last chosen weft yarn, and comb it up against the last plain woven line.

Finishing the Bookmark

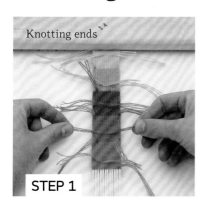

Knotting ends

STEP 1

Weaving in ends

Supergluing ends

Turn the loom over, and begin securing any loose yarn ends by either knotting them, weaving them back into the weaving, or supergluing them if necessary.

Though all of these finishing methods work, for bookmarks I sometimes use a very small amount of superglue. It's not always possible to weave the ends back into the weave—either because the weave is too tight and the yarn is too thick or short or because it would leave a large bump that shows through to the front of the bookmark.

STEP 2

Once the yarn ends are secured on the back, cut the bookmark off the loom on the bottom, leaving lots of space for the fringe.

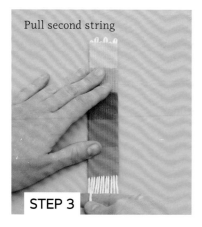

Pull second string

STEP 3

Pull fourth string

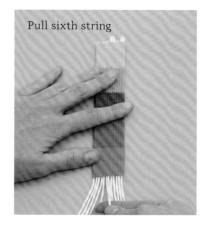

Pull sixth string

Lay the bookmark on a flat surface, and firmly press down on the woven area with one hand while slowly but *firmly* pulling every other warp string at the bottom, starting with the second string. Doing this will magically make the loops at the top of the bookmark disappear and slide down flush with the starting line.

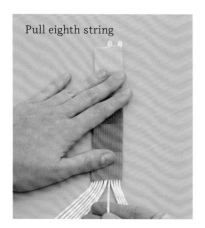

Pull eighth string

Pull tenth string

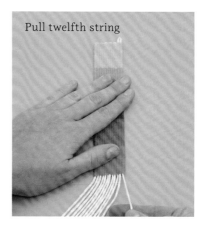

Pull twelfth string

TIP | BE SURE NOT TO PULL TOO FAST OR WITH TOO MUCH FORCE BECAUSE IF YOU PULL THE LOOP TOO FAR DOWN, DISTORTING THE STRAIGHT WOVEN LINE AT THE TOP OF THE BOOKMARK, IT WILL BE HARD TO PULL THE LOOP BACK UP!

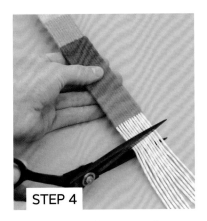

STEP 4

Finally, trim the fringe down to about 1″ (2.5cm) in length.

Now, test it out in your favourite book!

Photo by Isaac Vallentin

Woven Necklace

Tools & Materials

Weaving needle

Chenille needle

Measuring tape

Weaving comb

Scissors

Sewing pin

Warp yarn

3 selected weft yarns

Large frame loom, recommended 22″ × 28″ (55.9cm × 71.1cm)

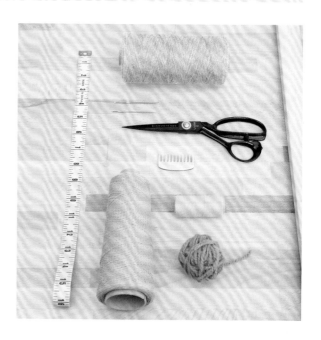

Notes on Project Materials and Sizing

I am using 100% linen slub from Weaver House for the warp of this project. Using a thinner warp fibre will help to make a flexible weaving, which is great for wearable weaves.

For the weft of this project, I'm using a small spool of thin 100% wool thread, a thicker wool yarn from a local farm here in Nova Scotia, and a thin 100% cotton weaving thread from Gist Yarn.

Use extra-long pieces of yarn measuring about 24″ (61cm) long to weave each section of weft in this project. This will help to minimize the amount of yarn ends that you will have to weave in on the back, which will result in a cleaner and flatter back side.

The length of the loom will determine how long the necklace can be. A large frame loom measuring 22″ × 28″ (55.9cm × 71.1cm) will make a necklace about 24″ (61cm) long. If you want to make a longer necklace using this design, you will need to use a longer loom.

This necklace will be sewn together at the end, so make sure that you measure the circumference of your head first, and plan to weave a necklace that will clear that measurement when it's folded in half so it fits over your head.

Techniques Needed for This Project

TWINING, page 56

PLAIN WEAVING, page 54

DOVETAILING, page 57

HAND SEWING, page 74

Photo by Isaac Vallentin

Making the Necklace

STEP 1

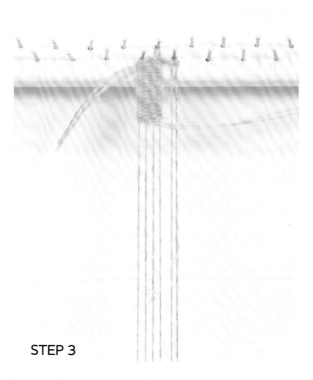

STEP 3

Warp the loom with six warp strings around three nails at the top of the frame (though the number of nails will depend on the loom), so the warped space measures about ½" (1.2cm) wide.

STEP 2: Weave a starting line in any of the chosen weft fibres, and push it up to the lower row of nails at the top of the loom with the comb.

Using the plain weave (1/1) technique and the same weft yarn that you wove the starting line with, weave across four warp strings, leaving two strings unwoven (besides the starting line). Continue plain weaving until the section is roughly ½" (1.2cm) long.

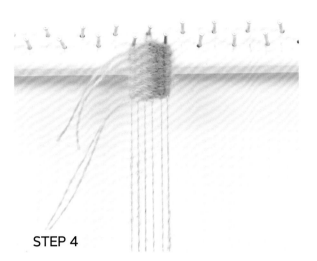

STEP 4

Using the second weft yarn, start on the right side of the warp, and weave across to meet the first weft yarn. Connect the two weft sections using the dovetailing technique. Weave down the same length as the first weft yarn.

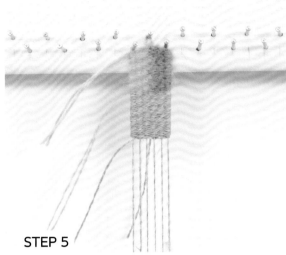

STEP 5

Using the third chosen weft yarn, plain weave for ½″ (1.2cm) across the entire warp.

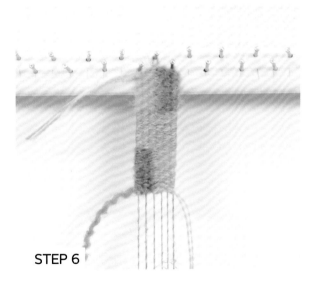

STEP 6

Repeat Steps 3-4, switching the order of the first two weft yarns. Then, repeat Step 5 with the third weft yarn.

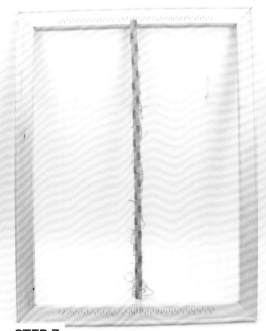

STEP 7

Repeat Steps 3-6 for the entire length of the warp, leaving 1″ (2.5cm) of warp space at the bottom of the loom.

STEP 8: Weave a finishing line, and then cut the necklace off the loom at the bottom, as close as possible to the nails on the bottom of the frame.

STEP 9

Secure all of the loose yarn ends on the back of the necklace. Have patience; this will take some time, but it'll be worth it! Do your best to weave in every yarn end, avoiding knotting and gluing as much as possible. Weaving all of the yarn ends in will make the back of the necklace feel soft and comfortable on your skin.

STEP 10

STEP 11

Fold the necklace in half, right side out with the ends together, and place a pin through both pieces where you want the necklace to attach.

Before you sew the pieces together, make sure that the necklace will fit over your head with them folded where you want to sew them.

Sew a few basic running stitches through both pieces using a chenille needle, using the same yarns as in the weft of the necklace, and then weave those yarn ends into the back so that they're hidden.

Try on the necklace, and see how it fits. The length and width of this simple necklace design can be easily adjusted to make a thicker or longer necklace or to make other accessories such as bracelets, headbands, and belts!

Photo by Isaac Vallentin

Coaster

Tools & Materials

Weaving needle

Scissors

2 selected warp yarns

2 selected weft yarns

Small frame loom,
recommended 11″ × 14″
(27.9cm × 35.5cm)

Notes on Project Materials

I'm using rug yarn from Balfour & Co for both the warp and the weft in this project. Normally I would say that's a no-no because wool is not generally a good type of fibre for warping due to its stretch, but this particular yarn is mixed with 20% nylon, which makes it stronger and less susceptible to stretching under tension pressure.

Use extra-long pieces of yarn measuring about 24″ (61cm) long to weave each section of weft in this project. This will help to minimize the amount of yarn ends that you will have to weave in on the back, which will result in a cleaner and flatter back side.

Techniques Needed for This Project

TWINING, page 56

TWILL WEAVE, page 55

Making the Coaster

To create a successful twill pattern, you should weave loosely enough so that you can see the warp strings behind the weft strings. For that reason, this project is a great exercise for practicing weft tension. You will need to feel the balance of weaving loosely (but not too loosely) while making sure that the edges stay parallel to each other.

You can use a needle to push weft lines up to make sure that they're straight, but you don't need to use a comb for this project.

STEP 1

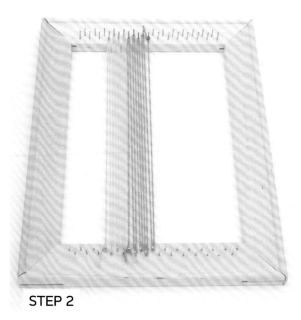

STEP 2

Warp the loom with eight warp strings using the first selected warp yarn. Tie the ends around a nail at the bottom of the loom.

Starting on the same nail that the first warp section ended on at the bottom of the loom, warp nine more strings using the second selected warp yarn. Tie the end around a nail at the top of the loom.

STEP 3

Starting on the same nail that the second warp section ended on at the top of the loom, warp nine more strings using the first selected warp yarn again. Tie the end around a nail at the bottom of the loom.

STEP 4

Complete the warp for your coaster by warping 9 more strings using the second chosen warp yarn, starting at the bottom of the loom with the same nail you ended on in Step 3. You should have a total of 35 warp strings.

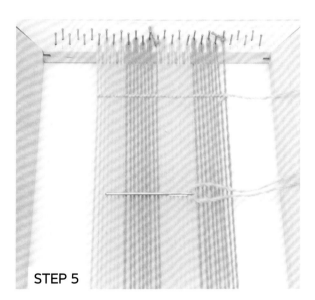

STEP 5

Weave a starting line in the first chosen weft yarn about 2″ (5.1cm) down from the nails at the top of the loom.

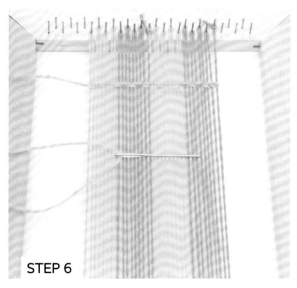

STEP 6

To begin the twill pattern, use the same yarn, and start from the right side. Weave under two warp strings then over two warp strings, and repeat all the way across the warp. You should finish the line on the left side with your weft yarn going over one warp string.

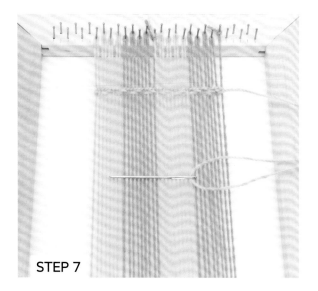

STEP 7

For the second woven line, start on the left, and weave over one, under one, over two, then under two; repeat the 2/2 pattern all the way across to the right side. You should finish the line by going over the last warp string.

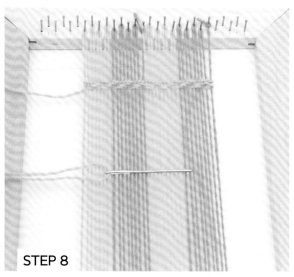

STEP 8

For the third woven line, start on the right, and weave under one, over one, under two, over two; repeat the 2/2 pattern all the way across. You should finish the line on the left by going under the last warp string.

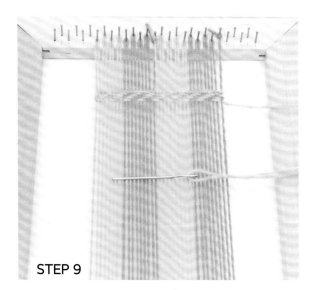

STEP 9

For the fourth woven line, start on the left, and weave the 2/2 pattern all the way across, finishing the line by going under the last warp string on the right.

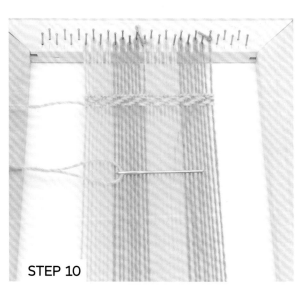

STEP 10

For the fifth woven line, start on the right, and weave over one, under one, over two, under two, continuing with the 2/2 pattern all the way across to the left side. You should finish the line by going over the last warp string.

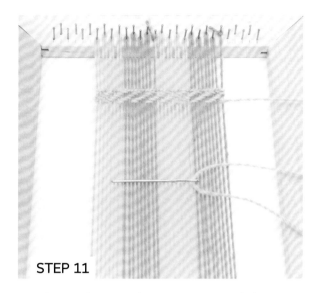

STEP 11

For the sixth woven line, start on the left, and weave the 2/2 pattern all the way across to the right side. You should finish the line by going over the last warp string.

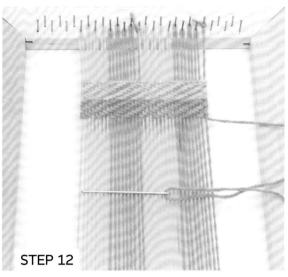

STEP 12

Repeat Steps 8-11 with the same colour weft yarn, and then change the weft yarn to the second chosen colour. Repeat Steps 8-11 twice with that colour. Your pattern should shift to the left by the same amount with each woven line.

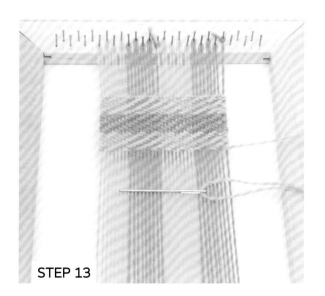

STEP 13

Change the weft yarn back to the first colour, and repeat Steps 8-11 twice.

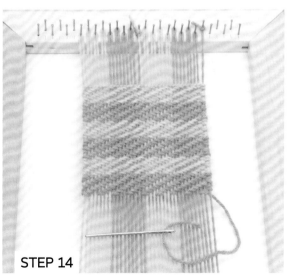

STEP 14

Change the weft yarn back to the second colour, and repeat Steps 8-11 twice. Continue switching weft yarn colours and repeating Steps 8-11 twice per colour until the coaster measures 4″ (10.2cm) long or however long you want the coaster to be.

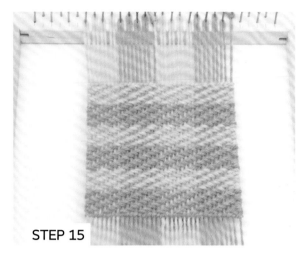

STEP 15

Weave a finishing line with the last-used weft yarn colour, and tuck the leftover yarn into the back so the tail sticks out on the back side.

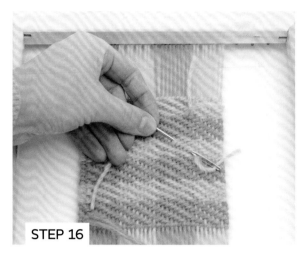

STEP 16

Turn the loom over, and weave all of the ends into the back of the weaving. Pull each end through at least three weft lines with the weaving needle in a diagonal direction. Try to match each end to the color and direction of the weft lines so that the ends do not stand out.

STEP 17

Cut the warp strings along the bottom of the loom. Unhook the loops from the top of the loom, and cut through them.

If the warp strings on the four corners of the coaster stick out or up, you can weave them into the back of the coaster just as you did with your loose yarn ends on the back for a flatter look.

STEP 18

Trim the fringe down to your desired length, but make it no shorter than ¾″ (1.9cm) to ensure that the weaving won't unravel.

These coasters make great gifts in pairs of two or sets of four and will last for years to come with gentle daily use. If they ever need cleaning, first try wiping them with a damp cloth. If that doesn't work, soak them in a bowl of cold water (if the yarns are wool) with a little bit of gentle detergent.

Photo by Isaac Vallentin

Tufted Brooch

Tools & Materials

Weaving needle

Comb

Measuring tape

Scissors

Thin warp yarn

Selected rya knot yarns measuring 3″ (7.6cm) long

Small frame loom, recommended 11″ × 14″ (27.9cm × 35.5cm)

Wooden brooch frame with inside area measuring 1″ (2.5cm)

Metal brooch pin

Hot glue gun

Hot glue sticks

Epoxy glue (optional)

Superglue

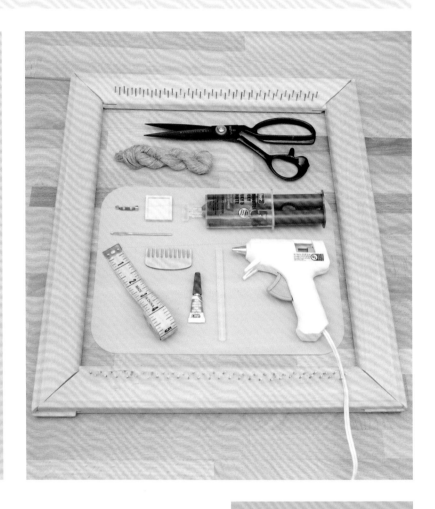

Notes on Project Materials

I'm using a strong and thin 100% linen slub from Weaver House for the warp of this project because the brooch is quite small. You want to maximize the amount of space for the rya knots by minimizing the amount of space occupied by the warp fibre. This results in a very densely knotted brooch.

The three materials listed below would work well for the warp of this project.

· 100% linen slub in Natural from Weaver House

· Aunt Lydia's 100% mercer-ized cotton crochet thread

· 8/4 unmercerized 100% cotton weaving yarn by Gist Yarn

Techniques Needed for This Project

TWINING, page 56

RYA KNOTS, page 58

I always use scrap yarn pieces when making rya knots for brooches because it's a great way to reuse materials and minimize waste in my practice. If you don't have any yarn scraps, you can use any yarns that measure between #1 and #4 on the yarn weight scale (page 16) and cut them into 3″ (7.6cm) long strips. This length is long enough to work with comfortably, but not so long that it will get in the way or create excessive waste.

Unless you are using yarns that are thinner than your warp yarn, it is always best to use fewer strands of yarn per knot and to have more knots than to have many strands per knot and fewer knots. This will ensure that the brooch will look full and dense when you trim it down later on. If you use more yarn per knot and make fewer knots, when you trim the brooch it won't look full, and the tops of the knots may show through.

I source my wooden brooch frames from an Etsy store called ArtWoodenSupply.

Scrap yarn pile I pull from for rya knots

The store has a great selection of brooch and pendant frames in a variety of shapes, sizes, and wood types. You might find brooch frames in your local craft supply stores or online with a bit of searching. Metal brooch pins can be found in your local craft and jewelry supply stores or online.

I prefer to use epoxy glue to affix the metal pin on the back of the brooch because I find that it creates a stronger and longer-lasting bond than hot glue does, but if you can't find epoxy glue, hot glue will work fine.

Making the Knotted Brooch Square

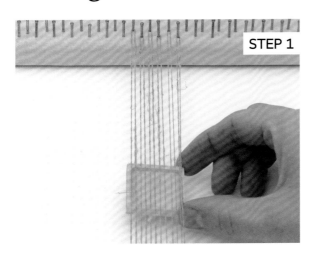

STEP 1

Warp the loom with twelve warp strings around six nails at the top of the frame (though the number of nails will depend on your loom) so the warped space measures about 1¼" (3.2cm). Hold the brooch frame behind the warp to make sure that the brooch tuft will fit inside the frame.

If you are using a larger or smaller brooch backing, you can adjust your warp based on its size, but it's important that you have an *even* number of warp strings because you need two strings to make each knot.

TIP | IF YOU CAN'T QUITE LINE UP THE INSIDE OF THE BROOCH BACKING WITH THE WIDTH OF THE WARP STRINGS, DON'T WORRY. YOU CAN REDUCE THE WIDTH OF THE WARP BY PULLING THE STRINGS CLOSER WHEN YOU WEAVE THE STARTING AND FINISHING LINES USING THE TWINING TECHNIQUE.

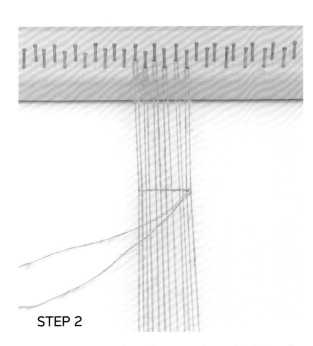

STEP 2

Weave a starting line, leaving about 3" (7.6cm) of warp space at the top of the loom.

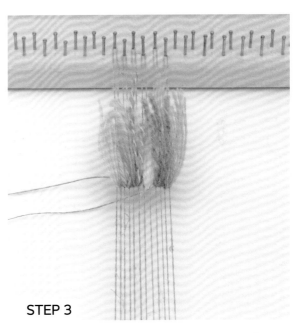

STEP 3

Using two or three pieces of weft yarn per knot, insert one line of rya knots with your fingers all the way across the warp, and push them up against the starting line.

STEP 4

Continue adding rya knots all the way across for about eight rows, until the weft measures ⅞" (2.2cm) in length. Be sure that the knots are pushed up together as much as possible so that you can fit as many knots within that length as possible. The denser the better.

STEP 5

Weave a finishing line under the last row of knots, and push it up tightly with your comb. The final length of the knotted tuft should measure ⅞" (2.2cm) in length or however long the inside of the brooch frame measures. Before continuing, again place the brooch behind the warp, and make sure the knots will fit.

STEP 6

Turn the loom over, and apply superglue to the sides of each knot and along the back of the starting and finishing line. This will keep the knots and lines in place when you're trimming it to fit into the brooch frame later on.

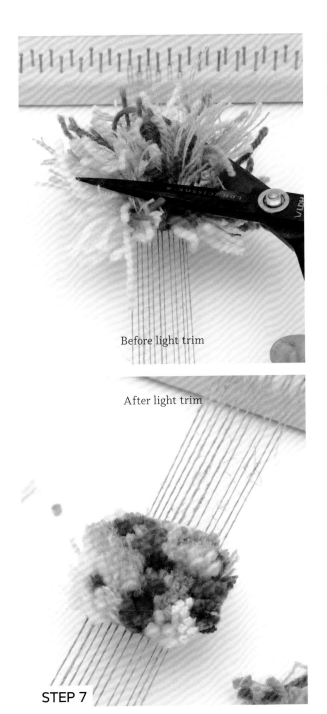

Before light trim

After light trim

STEP 7

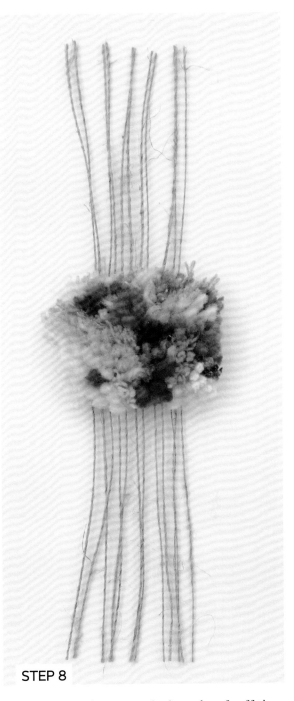

STEP 8

Turn the loom right side up, and give the rya knots a light trim. You will trim it again once it's in the brooch frame.

After the glue dries, cut the brooch tuft off the loom, leaving about 2″ (5.1cm) of warp string length on both sides.

Finishing the Brooch

STEP 1

Trim the warp threads down flush with the top and bottom of the tuft. Apply a bit more superglue to the starting and finishing lines to make sure that they won't unravel.

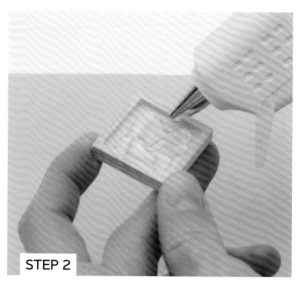

STEP 2

Apply hot glue to the inside of the wooden brooch frame, making sure you apply enough to reach the inside of each corner.

STEP 3

Quickly, before the glue dries, place the brooch tuft in the frame, paying extra attention to the corners and edges to ensure an even application of glue to the entire underside of the tuft.

STEP 4

Give the brooch tuft a final trim!

STEP 5

Apply a small amount of epoxy glue (or hot glue) to the back upper centre of the brooch, and place the metal brooch pin in the glue to set it. Rest the brooch tuft side down on a flat surface, and let it dry overnight (or for an hour or so if using hot glue).

Try it on to see how it looks!

Photo by Isaac Vallentin

Pillow

Tools & Materials

Weaving needle

Chenille needle

Sewing pins

Measuring tape

Weaving comb

Scissors

Warp yarn

2 selected weft yarns

Large frame loom, recommended 22″ × 28″ (55.9cm × 71.1cm)

Pillow insert **or** stuffing of choice (clumps of wool, yarn scraps, pillow stuffing, etc.)

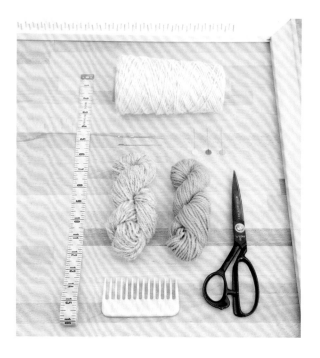

Notes on Project Materials

The recommended frame loom size for this project is based on a pillow insert measuring 12″ × 11″ (30.5cm × 27.9cm), ensuring that there will be plenty of loom space plus a bit extra to weave the pillow cover. You can weave a smaller pillow on a smaller loom if you'd like.

I'm using Balfour & Co rug yarns for this project. They are made from 80% wool and 20% nylon, which makes them sturdy and suitable to be used for both the warp and the weft. I'm weaving with consistent but relaxed tension and leaving a bit of space in between each woven line so that the warp shows through just a bit.

Techniques Needed for This Project

TWINING, page 56

PLAIN WEAVING, page 54

DOVETAILING, page 57

HAND SEWING, page 74

Making the Pillow

STEP 1

Warp the loom with 105 warp strings on about 52 nails at the top of the frame (though the number of nails will depend on your loom) so the warped space measures about 13″ (33cm) wide.

STEP 2

Weave a starting line using your first chosen yarn colour. Push the line up with the comb, leaving about 1″ (2.5cm) of warp space between it and the nails.

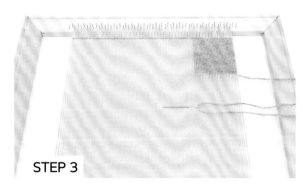

STEP 3

Starting from the top right side of the loom, and using either one of the two weft yarns, plain weave (1/1) toward the left side for 27 warp strings. Continue plain weaving back and forth on those 27 strings until the weft square measures 3¼″ long.

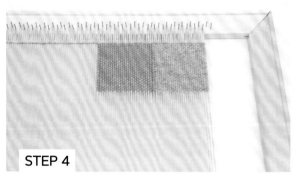

STEP 4

Cut a piece of the second weft yarn measuring about 20″ (50.8cm) long. On the 27 warp strings adjacent to the left of the first square, plain weave a second square connected to the first with the dovetailing technique. The shared warp string used for dovetailing should be included in the count of 27.

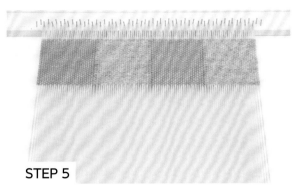

STEP 5

Switch back to the first weft colour, and weave another dovetailed square to the left of the second square for a width of 27 warp strings, including the warp string that is dovetailed to the previous square. Repeat this one more time for a fourth square using your second weft colour.

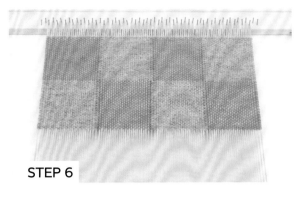

STEP 6

Continue weaving in the same way, repeating Steps 3-5 while reversing the colour pattern to create a second row of squares in a checkerboard design.

STEP 7

Repeat Steps 1-6 for the entire length of the warped loom. Leave roughly 1″ (2.5cm) of warp space at the bottom like you did at the top. Weave a finishing line.

STEP 8

Cut the weaving off of the loom at the bottom, cutting the warp strings as close to the frame of the loom as possible.

Flip the weaving over, and weave in all of the weft yarn ends.

STEP 9

STEP 10

Cut through the warp loops at the top of the weaving. Weave the leftover warp strings at the top and bottom into the back of the weaving just like you did with the yarn ends. Weave each warp string through at least three lines of weft, and then cut the ends flush to the weaving.

Fold the weaving in half, wrong side out, and cut a piece of one of your weft yarns measuring about 24″ (61cm) long. Thread a chenille needle with it. Starting on the top and bottom of the weaving where the warp strings are tucked, ¾″–½″ (1.9cm-1.2cm) away from the edge, sew the two layers together using a basic running stitch (page 74). Keep stitches close together, and pull them securely for a tightly sewn seam.

TIP | IF YOU WANT THE STITCHES TO BE HARD TO SEE, SWITCH BETWEEN THE WEFT YARNS TO MATCH THE CHECKERBOARD PATTERN WHILE SEWING. SEWING THROUGH EACH SQUARE USING ITS CORRESPONDING COLOUR OF YARN WILL KEEP YOUR STITCHES ALMOST INVISIBLE!

STEP 11

Sewing Side 2, leaving space for pillow insert

Once you've sewn the top and bottom edges together, do the same thing for one of the sides. For the remaining open side, start in one corner and sew about 2″ (5.1cm) toward the center. Switch to the other corner, and do the same. This leaves a gap about 6″ (15.2cm) wide, leaving enough room to fit a pillow insert in if it's folded in half. If you're filling your pillow with stuffing or wool scraps instead, you can leave a small hole to fill the pillow, about 2″ (5.1cm), which will make sewing the hole closed once it's flipped right side out very easy.

STEP 12

Turn the woven pillowcase right side out. If you're using a pillow insert, as shown, fold it in half, and slide it into the case opening. If you're using other stuffing, fill the inside of the pillow to your desired plushness.

STEP 13

Fold the edges of the gap under so no edges are showing, and then pin the opening closed.

STEP 14: Sew the hole closed with a ladder stitch (page 75). Switch between the weft yarns to match each square as you sew. Then weave all of the yarn ends into the seam to hide them, and trim them flush if need be.

Photo by Isaac Vallentin

This pillow project can be enjoyed at this scale as a small pop of pattern and colour or scaled up with a larger loom if you want something a little bigger to rest your head on.

Flat Gradient Wall Hanging

Tools & Materials

Weaving needle

Measuring tape

Weaving comb

Scissors

Warp yarn

5 selected weft yarns (4 in a colour gradient, 1 for the background)

Frame loom, recommended 14″ × 16″ (35.6cm × 40.6cm)

Wooden dowel measuring 8¼″ (21cm) long

Superglue (optional)

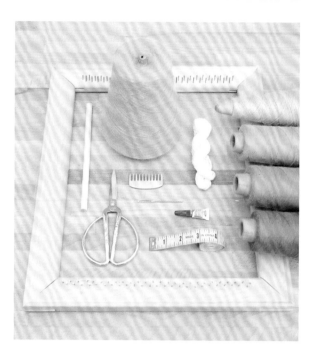

Notes on Project Materials

I'm using Patons Hempster 55% hemp and 45% cotton blend yarn for the warp of this project. The weight of this warp yarn is perfect for wall hangings that use the warp as fringe. It has a really nice organic and varied texture.

All of the weft yarns that I'm using for this project are #0 on the yarn weight scale (page 16). Since they're really thin, I've doubled them up to make them a little bit closer in weight to the warp yarn. This will ensure that I'm able to cover up the warp strings with ease as I weave. The background pink and the lightest peach yarns are thrifted wool cones, and the other three gradient weft yarns are from Gist Yarns's Array collection.

I cut the wooden dowel that I'm using for this project down to size with a small handsaw and sanded the ends with sandpaper. Wooden dowels can be found at your local craft supply, hardware, or dollar stores or online. You will almost always have to cut them down to size unless you are deciding the width of your wall hanging based on the length of a store-bought dowel.

Techniques Needed for This Project

TWINING, page 56

PLAIN WEAVING, page 54

SLIT, page 57

Making the Wall Hanging

STEP 1

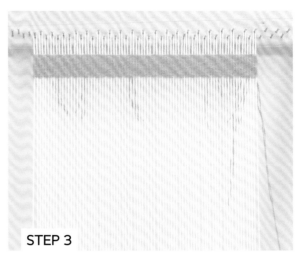

STEP 3

Plain weave (1/1) all the way across the warp until the weft measures a length of ¾″ (1.9cm).

Warp the loom with 80 warp strings over 40 nails at the top of the frame (though the number of nails will depend on your loom) so the warp space measures about 7.5″ (19.1cm).

STEP 2: Weave a starting line in the chosen background yarn colour. Push it up ½″ (1.2cm) from the nails at the top of your loom using the comb.

If you want to attach a wooden dowel by sewing it on at the end rather than feeding the dowel through loops at the top of the weaving, leave about 2″ (5.1cm) of warp space instead of just ½″ (1.2cm) between the starting line and the nails at the top of the loom. See page 72 in Chapter 7, Finishing Techniques, to see ways that you can attach a wooden dowel.

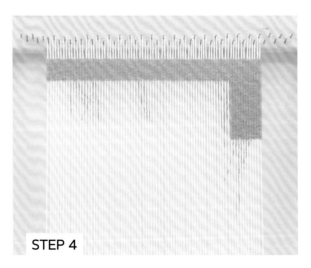

STEP 4

Using the same yarn and starting from the right side, weave back and forth across twelve warp strings until the rectangle of weft measures 2″ (5.1cm) in length.

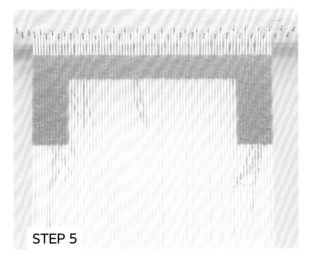

STEP 5

Repeat Step 4 on the left side of the warp.

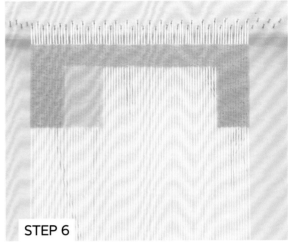

STEP 6

Cut a piece of the lightest chosen gradient yarn that measures about 24″ (61cm), and weave across fourteen warp strings, down 2″ (5.1cm). Start on the warp string next to the rectangle you wove in Step 5 on the left side of the warp. Use the slit technique between the two rectangles so that you have two clean colour edges that are not attached to each other. Continue using the slit technique for each new rectangle for the entire weaving.

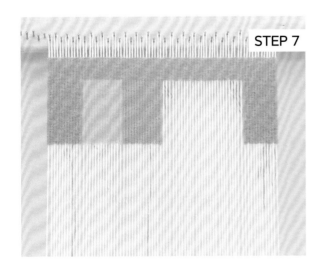

STEP 7

Repeat Step 6 using the next darkest gradient yarn, weaving across the fourteen warp strings to the right of the rectangle you wove in Step 6. When you finish the bottom line of the rectangle, look at the bottom line of the border rectangle to its left, and check to make sure that they both follow the correct over, under, over, under pattern. If they don't, you may need to weave one more line of your gradient colour or take one away.

Be sure to check this at the end of each following gradient rectangle so that you will be able to plain weave across the bottom of all of them with ease.

STEP 8: Repeat Step 6 using the third gradient yarn, weaving across the fourteen warp strings to the right of the rectangle you wove in Step 7.

STEP 9: Repeat Step 6 using the darkest gradient yarn, weaving across the fourteen warp strings to the right of the rectangle you wove in Step 8.

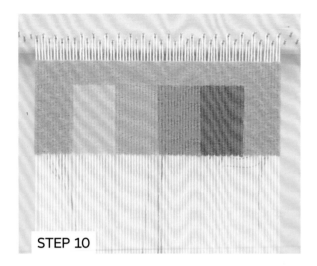

STEP 10

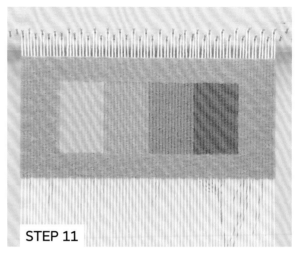

STEP 11

Use a measuring tape to make sure that all of the rectangles are the same approximate length. If some are a bit longer, use a comb to even them out. Turn the loom upside down to make sure you are weaving everything evenly and straight.

Switch back to the background yarn colour, and weave all the way across the warp until the section measures a length of ¾" (1.9cm).

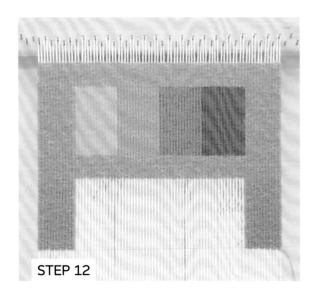

STEP 12

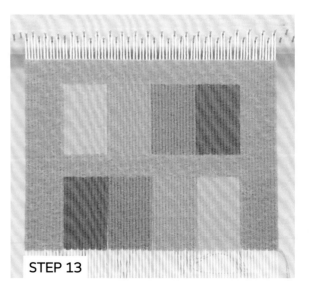

STEP 13

Repeat Steps 4–5.

Repeat Steps 6–9, reversing the gradient of yarn colours so that the darkest is on the left and the lightest is on the right.

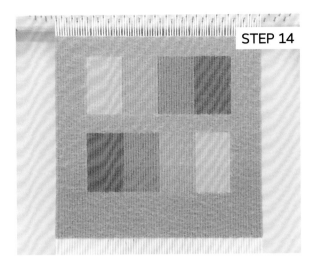

STEP 14

Switch back to the background color, and weave across the entire width of the warp until the length of the weft section measures 1¾" (4.4cm) long. Weave a finishing line along the bottom. The finishing line will secure the weft so that you can use the warp strings at the bottom as fringe without fearing that the weft will unravel.

STEP 15: Cut the weaving off of the loom as close to the bottom of the frame as you can.

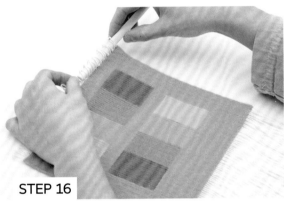

STEP 16

STEP 17

Feed a wooden dowel through all of the loops at the top of the weaving.

If the loops are different lengths and you want them all to be snug around the dowel, pull each of the longer loops upward, away from the dowel, and then down toward the back of the weaving. Hold them in place at the correct shorter length, and then attach them to the dowel with a small dab of superglue.

STEP 18: Weave in and/or tie off all of the yarn ends on the back of the weaving.

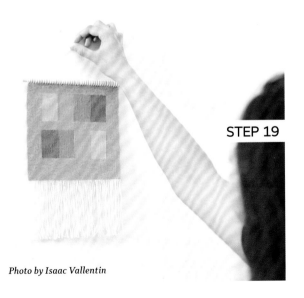

STEP 19

Attach a string to the dowel for hanging. Hang it on your wall, and enjoy the colour it adds to your space!

Photo by Isaac Vallentin

Circle and Square Puff Wall Hanging

Tools & Materials

Weaving needle

Measuring tape

Weaving comb

Scissors

Warp yarn

15-20 weft and rya knot yarns

Frame loom 11″ × 14″ (27.9cm 35.6cm)

Wooden dowel measuring 7″ (17.8cm) long

Superglue (optional)

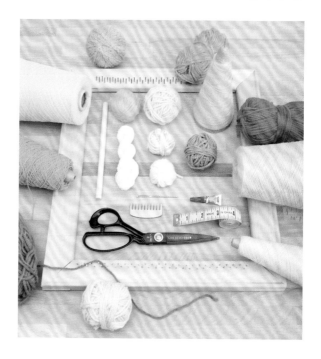

Notes on Project Materials

I'm using Patons Hempster 55% hemp and 45% cotton blend yarn for the warp of this project. The weft yarns that I'm using have all been thrifted over the years and vary in type of fibre. They are all roughly the same thickness/weight, between #1 and #3 on the yarn weight scale (page 16).

Using yarns that are all roughly the same weight for creating raised elements with rya knots will result in a finished piece on which the puffs all look similar in density. If you use thicker yarns for the knots of one raised shape and thinner yarns for another, the finished puffs will look different from one another after they're trimmed. All of the yarns used for the raised circles and squares were cut into 3″ (7.6cm) pieces prior to knotting.

I cut the wooden dowel that I'm using for this project down to size with a small handsaw and sanded the ends with sandpaper.

Techniques Needed for This Project

TWINING, page 56

PLAIN WEAVING, page 54

DOVETAILING, page 57

RYA KNOTS, page 58

Making the Wall Hanging

STEP 1

Warp the loom with 54 warp strings across 27 nails at the top of the frame (though the number of nails will depend on the loom) so the warp space measures approximately 6.25" (15.9cm).

STEP 2

Weave a starting line in the chosen background weft colour. Push it up to the top of the loom, leaving ½" (1.2cm) of warp space between it and the nails.

If you want to attach a wooden dowel by sewing it on at the end rather than feeding the dowel through loops at the top of the weaving, leave about 2" (5.1cm) of warp space instead of just ½" (1.2cm). See page 72 in Chapter 7, Finishing Techniques, to see ways that you can attach a wooden dowel.

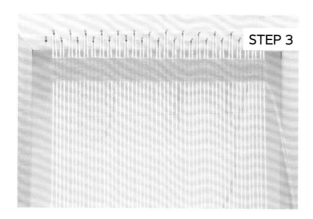

STEP 3

Plain weave (1/1) across the entire width of the warp until the weft measures a length of ¾" (1.9cm).

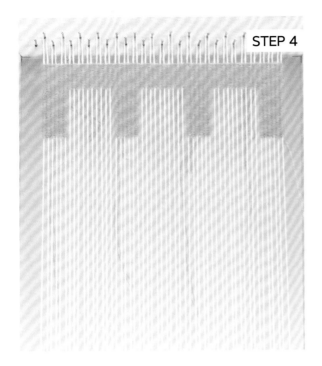

STEP 4

Plain weave a length of 1¼" (3.2cm) across six warp strings on both the right and left sides of the warp. Then, starting on the left edge of the rectangle on the right side of the warp, skip ten warp strings. Starting on the eleventh string, weave a length of 1¼" across six warp strings. Repeat the same step, this time starting on the right edge of the rectangle on the left side of the warp. This should leave three rectangles of open warp space with ten warp strings each.

The warp strings are divided as follows: six plain woven, ten empty, six plain woven, ten empty, six plain woven, ten empty, six plain woven. The tens will be raised circle and square puffs.

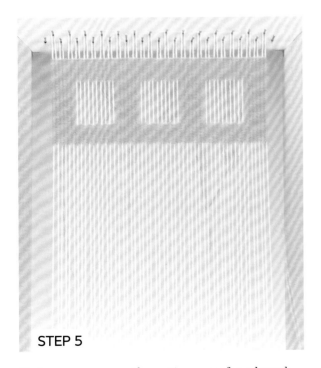

STEP 5

Plain weave across the entire warp for a length of ½" (1.2cm). This will complete the first row of open warp squares.

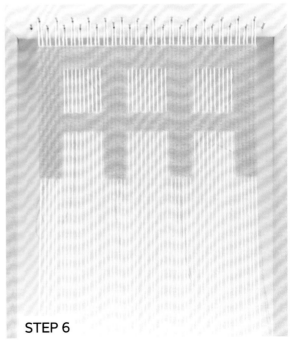

STEP 6

Repeat Step 4.

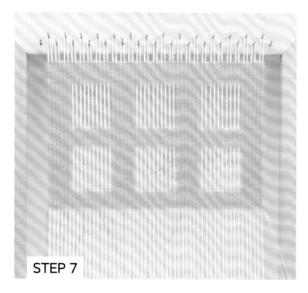

STEP 7

Repeat Step 5.

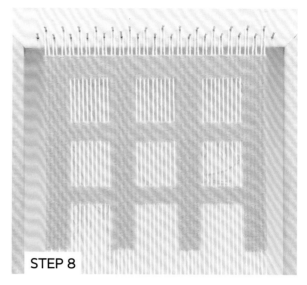

STEP 8

Repeat Step 4 one more time.

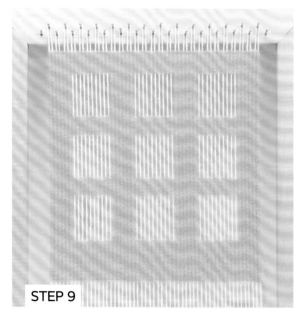

STEP 9

Plain weave across the entire width of the warp for a length of 1¼″ (3.2cm), and weave a finishing line at the bottom.

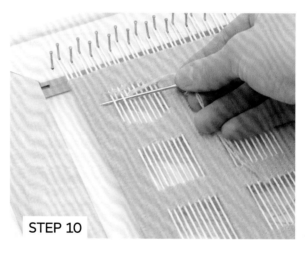

STEP 10

Now we're going to turn each of the corner open warp squares and the square in the center into circles. Start with the shape in the top left corner. Plain weave one line across five warp strings inside the shape, starting from the inner left edge of the flat-woven border.

For the second line, weave across four warp strings, three for the next, then two, and one. Use the dovetailing technique (see page 57) to connect these lines to the flat-woven section. Do this for all four corners of the open warp square to curve the corners into rounded edges.

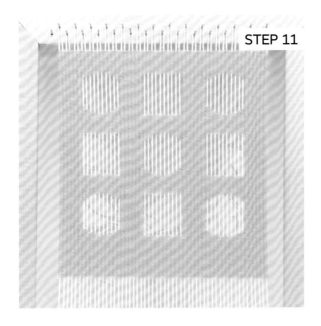

STEP 11 Repeat Step 10 on the other four selected shapes.

Top row: solid circle, gradient square, random knotted circle

Middle row: subtle checkerboard square, two-colour speckle circle, checkerboard stripe square

Bottom row: gradient circle, three-colour speckle square, gradient circle

STEP 12

Starting with the top left shape, fill in the open warp circles and squares with rya knots using your selected rya knot yarns.

Use any type of rya knot pattern (from Chapter 6, Rya Knots and Raised Elements, page 64) for each shape. See the patterns used for this project in the above captions.

STEP 13: Secure the knots on the back of the weaving (page 61).

STEP 14: Trim the rya knots on the front, tilting the loom periodically to make sure you're trimming them all down to the same height (unless you want them to be different heights).

TIP | DON'T BE AFRAID TO CHANGE THE COLOURS OR PATTERNS OF YOUR KNOTS IF YOU DON'T LIKE THEM ONCE THEY'RE TRIMMED. I DIDN'T LOVE HOW MUCH ATTENTION THE PINK CHECKERBOARD SQUARE WAS DEMANDING IN THE MIDDLE RIGHT SHAPE. SO I REMOVED THE KNOTS BY CUTTING THEM TO TRY SOMETHING A LITTLE MORE SUBDUED.

New knots inserted

Trimmed result

WHEN YOU'RE REMOVING RYA KNOTS THAT HAVE BEEN SECURED ON THE BACK, BE CAREFUL NOT TO CUT THE WARP STRINGS. CAREFULLY CUT THE WEFT LINES THAT YOU WOVE ON THE BACK OF THE KNOTS TO SECURE THEM. REMOVE THE KNOTS BY PICKING THEM OUT WITH THE HELP OF YOUR WEAVING NEEDLE.

FILL THE WARP STRINGS BACK UP WITH NEW KNOTS, AND SECURE THEM AGAIN ON THE BACK BEFORE YOU TRIM THEM.

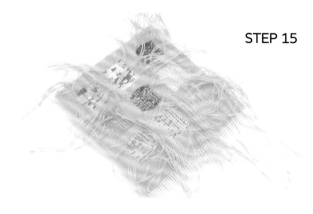

STEP 15 Cut the weaving off the loom as close to the bottom of the frame as possible.

STEP 16: Weave in or tie off all of the loose yarn ends on the back.

STEP 17 Attach a wooden dowel by feeding it through the loops at the top. If the loops are different lengths and you want them all to be snug around the dowel, pull each of the longer loops upward away from the dowel and then down toward the back of the weaving. Hold them in place at the correct shorter length, and then attach them to the dowel with a small dab of superglue.

STEP 18: Attach a string to the dowel for hanging. Hang it on a wall where you can enjoy its texture from every angle.

Photo by Isaac Vallentin

About the Author

Allyson Rousseau is a Canadian artist and weaver.

She earned her bachelor of arts degree in studio art from the University of Guelph in 2014, where she took a variety of studio courses including painting, welding, and woodworking. The absence of a textile department at the time left her to her own self-teaching, which she has since developed into a full-time artistic practice.

After several years of weaving for her own learning and exploration, Allyson began her journey as a teacher with the release of her five online video classes. In the summer of 2022, she celebrated the release of her first Domestika course entitled 3D Weaving & Yarn Trimming for Wall Hangings.

She has exhibited her work in Canada, the United States, and Europe and has created hundreds of custom pieces for clients all over the world. Her work has been featured in numerous national and international publications including two books: *Weaving: Contemporary Makers on the Loom* in 2018 and *Woven Together: Weavers & Their Stories* in 2020.

Photo by Isaac Vallentin

Allyson currently lives with her partner Isaac in the sleepy little port town of Pictou, Nova Scotia.

Find her online at allysonrousseau.com.

CREATIVE SPARK
ONLINE LEARNING

Crafty courses to become an expert maker...

From their studio to yours, Creative Spark instructors are teaching you how to create and become a master of your craft. So not only do you get a look inside their creative space, you also get to be a part of engaging courses that would typically be a one or multi-day workshop from the comfort of your home.

Creative Spark is not your one-size-fits-all online learning experience. We welcome you to be who you are, share, create, and belong.

Scan for a gift from us!

creativespark.ctpub.com